Intellectual Property Law in New Zealand

Intellectual Property Law in New Zealand

Anna Kingsbury

This book was originally published as a monograph in the International Encyclopaedia of Laws/Intellectual Property Law.

Founding Editor: Roger Blanpain
General Editor: Frank Hendrickx
Volume Editor: Hendrik Vanhees

Wolters Kluwer

Published by:
Kluwer Law International B.V.
PO Box 316
2400 AH Alphen aan den Rijn
The Netherlands
Website: www.wklawbusiness.com

Sold and distributed in North, Central and South America by:
Wolters Kluwer Legal & Regulatory U.S.
7201 McKinney Circle
Frederick, MD 21704
United States of America
Email: customer.service@wolterskluwer.com

Sold and distributed in all other countries by:
Turpin Distribution Services Ltd.
Stratton Business Park
Pegasus Drive, Biggleswade
Bedfordshire SG18 8TQ
United Kingdom
Email: kluwerlaw@turpin-distribution.com

Printed on acid-free paper

ISBN 97890-411-8749-9

e-Book: ISBN 97890-411-8772-7
web-PDF: ISBN 97890-411-8802-1

This title is available on www.kluwerlawonline.com

Printed and Bound by CPI Group (UK) Ltd, Croydon, CR0 4YY.

The Author

Prof. Dr Anna Kingsbury was born in Wellington, New Zealand. She obtained a Bachelor of Arts degree in History and Politics from the University of Auckland and a Bachelor of Laws from Victoria University of Wellington. She also has a Masters in Law from the University of Melbourne, a Masters in Law specializing in Trade Regulation from New York University, and a Doctorate in Juridical Science from La Trobe University. She has been admitted as a Barrister and Solicitor of the High Court of New Zealand. She has taught in the Faculty of Law at the University of Waikato since 1997, where she teaches the law of intellectual property as well as the law of torts and competition law. She has published widely in the area of Intellectual Property Law, both in New Zealand and internationally.

The Author

Table of Contents

List of Abbreviations

APRA	Australasian Performing Rights Association
IPONZ	Intellectual Property Office of New Zealand
NZ	New Zealand
P	page
S	section
Ss	Sections
TRIPS	Agreement on Trade Related Aspects of Intellectual Property Rights 1994
UK	United Kingdom
US	United States
V	Volume

General Introduction

§1. General Background

I. Geography

1. New Zealand is a small island nation located in the south-western Pacific Ocean. It lies about 1,600 km from Australia, and occupies 269,652 sq km. It is made up of two large islands, known as the North Island and the South Island, and a number of smaller islands, the largest of which is Stewart Island to the south. The South Island (150,437 sq km) is larger than the North Island (113,729 sq km). Stewart Island is 1,680 sq km. The three main islands stretch 1,500 km across latitudes 34° to 47° south.[1]

The Māori name for New Zealand is Aotearoa, and although not designated as the official name of the country, this name is also in common use. For the main islands of New Zealand, both English and Māori names were designated in 2013 as alternative official names. The Māori name for the North Island is Te Ika-a-Māui, and the South island is Te Waipounamu.

II. Cultural Composition

2. The Māori people were the first inhabitants of New Zealand, but Māori are now a minority of the population as a result of colonization and immigration. New Zealand was a colony of Great Britain, and much of the European (or pakeha) population is descended from British migrants. Migrants also came from the Pacific Island nations. However, sources of migration have in recent years become increasingly diverse.

New Zealand has a population of approximately 4.4 million people. The 2013 census data on ethnicity shows the composition of the population. Nearly three-quarters of the population (74%) identified themselves as being of European ethnicity, and 14.9% identified themselves as belonging to the Māori ethnic group. Pacific peoples were 7.4%, and 11.8% identified themselves as Asian. A total of 1.2% identified as Middle Eastern, Latin American or African, and 1.7% were in the 'other ethnicity'

1. Ministry for Culture and Heritage: Manatū Taonga, *Te Ara–The Encyclopedia of New Zealand*, http://www.teara.govt.nz/en/natural-environment/page-1 (accessed 25 Mar. 2014).

category. Note that in the census data, people were able to identify with more than one ethnic group and therefore percentages do not add up to 100.[2]

New Zealand has three official languages, English, Te Reo Māori and New Zealand Sign Language. English is the most commonly used language. Around one-quarter of Māori are fluent Māori speakers.[3] Of the population as a whole, 3.7% speak Māori.[4]

III. Political System

3. New Zealand's political system is a representative democracy and constitutional monarchy. There are three branches of government, the Parliament, the executive and the judiciary.

The Head of State is Queen Elizabeth II, the Governor-General is her representative appointed on the advice of the New Zealand government. The Parliament is comprised of the Governor-General and the elected House of Representatives. The New Zealand House of Representatives is elected every three years under a mixed member proportional system. The Parliament is based on the Westminster model, but is unicameral. The doctrine of parliamentary supremacy applies.

The executive is the administrative branch of government. It is comprised of the Governor-General, the Prime Minister and Cabinet, government departments and the public service, local government, state-owned enterprises and various statutory bodies. The judiciary is independent of government.

IV. Population Statistics

4. The population of New Zealand is approximately 4.4 million people. The population is increasing. Between the census of 2006 and the census of 2013, the population grew by over 5%. Around three-quarters of the population live in the North Island, with just over 1 million in the South island. Auckland, in the upper North Island, is the largest city with 1.4 million people. Auckland is also the fastest growing city.

§2. Historical Background

5. The first occupants of Aotearoa/New Zealand were the Polynesian settlers who became known as Māori. Māori discovered Aotearoa in the course of their

---

2. Statistics New Zealand, Tatauranga Aotearoa, *2013 Census QuickStats about National Highlights: Cultural Diversity*, http://www.stats.govt.nz/Census/2013-census/profile-and-summary-reports/quickstats-about-national-highlights/cultural-diversity.aspx (accessed 25 Mar. 2014).
3. Ministry of Social Development, *The Social Report 2010*, at 88, http://www.socialreport.msd.govt.nz/documents/the-social-report-2010.pdf (accessed 25 Mar. 2014).
4. Statistics New Zealand, Tatauranga Aotearoa, *2013 Census QuickStats about National Highlights: Cultural Diversity*, http://www.stats.govt.nz/Census/2013-census/profile-and-summary-reports/quickstats-about-national-highlights/cultural-diversity.aspx (accessed 25 Mar. 2014).

expeditions of exploration from Polynesia. The navigator Kupe is credited with finding the land masses now known as New Zealand. The first arrivals by Māori people are generally understood to have taken place in the thirteenth century.

European explorers first became aware of the existence of New Zealand in 1642 when the Dutch explorer Abel Tasman charted part of the coast. The next European explorer to arrive was James Cook in 1769. Small numbers of European settlers settled in New Zealand in ensuing years, and the British made moves to formally adopt a governance role.

In 1840, the Treaty of Waitangi was signed between Māori leaders (chiefs) and the British Crown. The Treaty of Waitangi is regarded as a founding document of New Zealand although its meaning has been a source of dispute over many years, partly as a result of differences between the English and Māori texts. The terms of the Treaty have also frequently been breached by the Crown.

After 1840, New Zealand became a Crown colony. British settlement significantly increased, and the New Zealand Constitution Act of 1852 was passed by the British Parliament, setting up self-government for the British settlers in New Zealand. British law was transplanted to New Zealand, and the New Zealand Constitution and system of government is still based on the British system. At the same time, from the 1850s onward, there were growing disputes over land sales, as Māori declined to sell land the British settlers wanted. Wars between settlers and Māori followed in the 1860s, and Māori resistance was largely overcome by force. Settler law was largely imposed on Māori. Large areas of land were then confiscated from Māori owners, and systems for further alienation of land were established.

In the years that followed, New Zealand developed from its status as a colony. In 1907, New Zealand became a dominion, and in 1947, New Zealand adopted the Statute of Westminster and accepted full autonomy from Britain. In 1949, New Zealand citizenship came into existence. Voting rights were also gradually extended. Universal suffrage for men over 21 was introduced in 1879 and for women in 1893.

In the period after the second world war, Māori migration to the cities increased, as did Māori political influence. Māori leaders were increasingly assertive about grievances over the treatment of Māori, the confiscation of land, and the many breaches of the Treaty of Waitangi by the Crown. In response to calls from Māori, the Waitangi Tribunal was established in 1975 to address grievances from 1975 onwards, but not historic grievances. In 1985, the Tribunal was empowered to look at breaches of the treaty since 1840 rather than since 1975.

The Waitangi Tribunal continues to hear and report on claims of treaty breaches. Most significantly, for intellectual property law was the 'Wai-262' claim which was one of the most complex claims dealt with by the Tribunal. It was referred to as the intellectual property claim. It concerned who controls Māori traditional knowledge, artistic and cultural works and the environment, including the flora and fauna, that created Māori culture. The Waitangi Tribunal reported on this claim in 2011, making a number of recommendations, and the Government is yet to respond.[5]

Other notable events in recent New Zealand political history include the passage of the New Zealand Bill of Rights Act in 1990, and a change to mixed member

5. *Ko Aotearoa Tēnei: A Report into Claims Concerning New Zealand Law and Policy Affecting Māori Culture and Identity*: Wai 262, Waitangi Tribunal Report 2011.

proportional voting used for the first time in 1996. In 2003, the Supreme Court Act was passed, which replaced the Privy Council in London with a New Zealand Supreme Court as the court of final appeal.

Chapter 1. Copyright and Neighbouring Rights

§1. Sources: Legislation

6. New Zealand copyright law has a statutory basis in the Copyright Act 1994. Historically, New Zealand copyright law has evolved from English copyright law, with New Zealand copyright legislation traditionally being based on that in the United Kingdom (UK). This trend has continued, with the New Zealand Copyright Act 1994 being largely modelled on the United Kingdom Copyright, Designs and Patents Act 1988, but with some very significant differences. The New Zealand legislation is significantly different from Australian copyright law, despite the proximity and similarities between the two countries. As is the situation in all jurisdictions, international agreements on copyright are of growing importance in copyright law.

Legislation

The principal statute is the Copyright Act 1994
The main regulations in this field are:

- Copyright (Application to Other Countries) Order 1995.
- Copyright (Border Protection) Regulations 1994.
- Copyright (General Matters) Regulations 1995.
- Copyright (Infringing File Sharing) Regulations 2011.

In addition to the Copyright Act 1994 and regulations, there is a growing body of New Zealand case law interpreting the copyright legislation. Where relevant, New Zealand courts also refer to copyright case law from other jurisdictions, not only particularly from the UK, but also from jurisdictions such as Australia, Canada and the United States (US).

§2. Subject Matter of Protection

I. Different Categories of Protected Works

7. The categories of works protected under the Copyright Act 1994 are set out in section 14. Section 2 provides that a 'copyright work' means a work of any of the descriptions in section 14(1) in which copyright exists. Section 14 of the Copyright Act 1994 provides:

14. Copyright in original works —

> 1. Copyright is a property right that exists, in accordance with this Act, in original works of the following descriptions:
>
> (a) literary, dramatic, musical, or artistic works:
> (b) sound recordings:
> (c) films:
> (d) communication works:
> (e) typographical arrangements of published editions.
> 2. A work is not original if—
> it is, or to the extent that it is, a copy of another work; or
> it infringes the copyright in, or to the extent that it infringes the copyright in, another work.

8. Section 2 of the Copyright Act is the Interpretation section. It provides definitions of some of the terms used in section 14. Particular aspects of the definitions and characteristics of the works are described as follows:

A. Literary Works

9. The term 'literary work' in section 14 is defined in section 2 as meaning:

> any work, other than a dramatic or musical work, that is written, spoken, or sung; and includes—

(a) a table or compilation; and
(b) a computer program.

Section 2 provides that 'writing' includes any form of notation or code, whether by hand or otherwise and regardless of the method by which, or medium in or on which, it is recorded; and written has a corresponding meaning.

A literary work is therefore a work that is not a dramatic or musical work that is written, spoken or sung. Compilations are included and this includes compilations of data, giving important protection to works such as databases, although the 'compilation' category is much wider than that. Section 2 defines 'compilation' to include:

(a) a compilation consisting wholly of works or parts of works; and
(b) a compilation consisting partly of works or parts of works; and
(c) a compilation of data other than works or parts of works.

Under the Copyright Act 1994, computer programs are also protected by copyright as literary works.

There is substantial case law on the meaning of literary work. It is well established that there is no requirement of literary quality of style.[6] Literary works are generally required to afford 'either information and instruction, or pleasure in the form of literary enjoyment'.[7] Most works that are written, spoken or sung will qualify. Some works will not qualify, however, either because they are not original enough, or because they do not meet the requirements for a 'literary work'. For example, invented words,[8] titles[9] and some slogans[10] have been found not to qualify as original literary works. There is continuing uncertainty about slogans and headlines. In a recent New Zealand High Court decision, the Judge found, surprisingly, that the advertising slogan 'Field Friendly – the best choice for field work' was an original literary work protected by copyright. In a recent Australian case, the court found against copyright in newspaper headlines.[11] By contrast, a recent English case found that there was copyright in headlines.[12] There remains therefore some uncertainty about whether these kinds of work qualify as literary works, and as to whether they are original enough, and this is still to be resolved by New Zealand courts.

B. Dramatic Works

10. Dramatic works are defined in section 2 to include a work of dance or mime; and a scenario or script for a film. The definition is inclusive, so that other works, such as plays, are also included. If a work is a dramatic work, it cannot be a literary work. Dramatic works are generally works that can be acted or performed.[13] A dramatic work

---

6. In *University of London Press v. University Tutorial Press Ltd* [1916] 2 Ch 601, 608 Peterson J observed that copyright protects books and also many things with no pretensions to literary style, such as trade catalogues. 'In my view the words "literary work" cover work which is expressed in print or writing, irrespective of the question whether the quality or style is high. The word "literary" seems to be used in a sense somewhat similar to the use of the word "literature" in political or electioneering literature and refers to written or printed matter.' *See also Ladbroke (Football) Ltd v. William Hill (Football) Ltd* [1964] 1 WLR 273; [1964] 1 All ER 465 (HL).
7. *Exxon Corporation v. Exxon Insurance Consultants International Ltd* [1981] 3 All ER 241; 248.
8. *Exxon Corporation v. Exxon Insurance Consultants International Ltd* [1981] 3 All ER 241; [1982] RPC 69.
9. For example the words 'Opportunity Knocks' in *Green v. Broadcasting Corporation of New Zealand* [1988] 2 NZLR 490 (CA); [1989] 3 NZLR 18 (PC); (1989) 16 IPR 1, the novel title 'Splendid Misery' in *Dicks v. Yates* (1881) 18 Ch D 76. *See also Francis Day Hunter v. 20th Century Fox* [1940] AC 112.
10. For example, the slogan 'Youthful appearance is a social necessity, not a luxury' was refused protection in *Sinanide v. La Maison Kosmeo* (1928) 139 LTR 365. The issue of whether copyright can exist in slogans was left open in *No Fear Inc v. Farmers Trading Co Ltd*, Unreported, High Court, Auckland, M1616/95, 31 Aug. 1998, Morris J.
11. *Fairfax Media Publications Pty Ltd v. Reed International Books Australia Pty Ltd* [2010] FCA 984.
12. *The Newspaper Licensing Agency Ltd v. Meltwater Holding Bv* [2011] EWCA Civ 890, [2012] RPC 1.
13. *Green v. Broadcasting Corp of NZ* [1988] 2 NZLR 490 (CA), 497.

'must have sufficient unity to be capable of performance'.[14] A dramatic work has also been described as 'a work of action, with or without words or music, which is capable of being performed before an audience'.[15]

C. Musical Works

11. Under the section 2 definition, a musical work 'means a work consisting of music, exclusive of any words intended to be sung or spoken with the music or any actions intended to be performed with the music'. The musical work is therefore the music. Words or actions intended to accompany the music may be protected separately as literary or dramatic works. Thus a work such as a song may be protected as a musical work, a literary work and potentially also as a sound recording.

D. Artistic Works

12. New Zealand copyright law is unusual in the range or works protected by copyright under the artistic works category. A variety of works are covered that would be excluded or subject to a design right in other jurisdictions. The section 2 definition of artistic work in the Copyright Act 1994 is as follows:

artistic work:

(a) means—

(i) a graphic work, photograph, sculpture, collage, or model, irrespective of artistic quality; or

(ii) a work of architecture, being a building or a model for a building; or

(ii) a work of artistic craftsmanship, not falling within subparagraph (i) or subparagraph (ii); but

(b) does not include a layout design or an integrated circuit within the meaning of section 2 of the Layout Designs Act 1994.

There are therefore three categories of artistic work under the definition. In practice, the definition of 'artistic works' covers a wide range of things, including things that would not generally be regarded as artistic. Any work that is covered by one of the categories of artistic work is protected. This includes drawings, diagrams and plans which are protected as graphic works, and prototypes protected as models.[16] A number

14. *Green v. Broadcasting Corp of NZ* [1988] 2 NZLR 490 (CA), [1989] 3 NZLR 18 (PC), 20.
15. *Norowzian v. Arks Ltd* (No 2) [1999] EWCA Civ 3014.
16. *See* for example, *Thornton Hall Manufacturing Ltd v. Shanton Apparel Ltd (No 2)* [1989] 1 NZLR 234.

of the types of works within the artistic work definition are also separately defined in section 2. 'Graphic work' is defined as including: '(a) any painting, drawing, diagram, map, chart, or plan; and (b) any engraving, etching, lithograph, woodcut, print, or similar work'. This category of graphic works is particularly significant in offering protection to a wide range of industrial design products, including functional products. Included are a range of items used in industry, including drawings, diagrams and plans as well as three-dimensional items. This category of works has been used to protect items including fashion designs,[17] furniture designs[18] and packaging.[19] For the purposes of industry, particularly important categories of artistic work are 'graphic work', 'model' and 'work of artistic craftsmanship', which is not defined.[20] A work may also qualify as a sculpture.[21] Section 2 defines 'sculpture' as including a cast or model made for purposes of sculpture. Buildings and plans for buildings are also protected. Plans will be protected as graphic works, and buildings that are works of architecture are also protected. Section 2 defines 'building' as including '(a) any fixed structure; and (b) a part of a building or fixed structure.'

For the first group of works in the definition of artistic works (graphic works, photographs, sculptures, collages, or models), the provision specifically provides that they are included 'irrespective of artistic quality'. There is no 'irrespective of artistic quality' provision in the second and third limbs of the definition. This omission suggests that for these works, there may be some requirement of artistic quality. Thus, there may be an aesthetic requirement for works of architecture, being a building or a model for a building, and works of artistic craftsmanship.

The category of works of artistic craftsmanship is particularly important for industrial design. 'Work of artistic craftsmanship' is a category of works that was introduced to give protection to works of art other than those specifically included by name in the definition of artistic work. Its purpose was to provide protection for traditional crafts, such as the work of silversmiths, potters, woodworkers and embroiderers. These craftspeople especially needed protection where their work did not involve sketches that could have been protected as graphic works. The term 'work of artistic craftsmanship' is not defined in the Act. It is a category that covers a very wide variety of works. Works of artistic craftsmanship are required to have some artistic quality. According to Tipping J in *Bonz Group (Pty) Ltd v. Cooke:*[22]

> [F]or a work to be regarded as one of artistic craftsmanship it must be possible fairly to say that the author was both a craftsman and an artist. A craftsman is a person who makes something in a skilful way and takes justified pride in their workmanship. An artist is a person with creative ability who produces something which has aesthetic appeal.

---

17. *Thornton Hall Manufacturing Ltd v. Shanton Apparel Ltd (No 2)* [1989] 1 NZLR 234, *Jeanswest Corporation (New Zealand) Ltd v. G-Star Raw C.V.* [2015] NZCA 14.
18. *Burden & Ors v. ESR Group & Ors* [2016] NZHC 1542.
19. *Henkel KgaA v. Holdfast New Zealand Ltd* [2006] NZSC 102, [2007] 1 NZLR 577.
20. *See* for example, *Bonz Group (Pty) Ltd v. Cooke* [1994] 3 NZLR 216.
21. *See* for example, *Wham-O MFG Co v. Lincoln Industries Ltd* [1984] 1 NZLR 641.
22. [1994] 3 NZLR 216, 224.

This approach was recently applied in *Dreamtech Designs & Productions Pty Ltd v. Clownfish entertainment Ltd & Ors.*[23] The High Court considered copyright in an attraction involving a series of maze-like rooms, each containing special effects and illusions, and found that there was an arguable case that it was a work of artistic craftsmanship.

E. Sound Recordings

13. Under section 2, 'sound recording' means either: '(a) a recording of sounds, from which the sounds may be reproduced; or (b) a recording of the whole or any part of a literary, dramatic, or musical work, from which sounds reproducing the work or part may be produced, regardless of the medium on which the recording is made or the method by which the sounds are reproduced or produced'. The first part of the definition covers actual recordings of sounds whether or not they are 'musical' or meaningful. It will include such things as recordings of birdsong. The second part of the definition covers recordings of literary, dramatic or musical works and includes things not recordings of sounds, such as electronic recordings from which sounds can be reproduced. What copyright protects is the sounds produced. The definition also includes film soundtracks. Under section 5(2)(b), the author of a sound recording is 'the person by whom the arrangements necessary for the making of the recording… are undertaken'.

F. Films

14. Under section 2, a film means 'a recording on any medium from which a moving image may by any means be produced'. Under section 5(2)(b), the author of a film is 'the person by whom the arrangements necessary for the making of the…film are undertaken'. This generally means that the author is the producer or production company, although there may be some difficulties where there are collaborative arrangements.

G. Communication Works

15. Section 2 defines 'communication work' as meaning 'a transmission of sounds, visual images, or other information, or a combination of any of those, for reception by members of the public, and includes a broadcast or a cable programme'. Sections 2 and 3 have a number of associated definitions. The category 'communication works' was introduced into the Copyright Act in 2008. It is designed to be a technology neutral replacement for the former two categories, 'broadcasts' and 'cable programmes'.

H. Typographical Arrangements of Published Editions

16. This copyright refers to the image of the work on the page; it protects the publisher's layout of the work. The copyright in the typographical arrangement exists independently of the copyright in the work itself. It is thus possible to have copyright

23. [2015] NZHC 1143.

in the typographical arrangement of a new edition of a work, even though the work itself may be very old and out of copyright. 'Typographical arrangement' is not defined in the Act, but 'published edition' means 'a published edition of the whole or any part of one or more literary, dramatic, or musical works'.

II. Works Excluded from Protection

17. Section 14 of the Copyright Act 1994 sets out the categories of work protected by copyright. There is no equivalent list of works excluded from protection. However, works may be excluded from protection for reasons such as:

(a) they are not covered by one of the categories in section 14; or
(b) they do not meet the other requirements for copyright to subsist in the work, such as originality, recording, or qualifying factors; or
(c) the subject matter is only an idea rather than an expression of an idea.

One category of works that has caused some difficulties for the courts is that of television formats. Television formats cannot be protected by copyright unless they meet the requirements of a literary or dramatic work, and this will depend on the facts. On some facts, television formats have been held not to qualify as literary or dramatic works because they are mere ideas for a television show, and lack sufficient certainty of subject matter. *See* for example *Green v. Broadcasting Corp of NZ*[24] where a format for a television talent quest was held on the facts to lack sufficient unity to be a dramatic work, and the scripts were not a literary work as they did not do more than express a general idea or concept.

III. Special Categories of Works

A. Computer Software

18. Before the enactment of the Copyright Act 1994, there was some doubt as to whether New Zealand copyright law protected computer programs. The Copyright Act 1962 made no reference to computer software. In the case *International Business Machines Corp v. Computer Imports Ltd*,[25] the Court held that the source code (human readable code) for a computer program was protectable by copyright as a literary work. The object code could not be an original literary work in its own right, because it was not in print or writing, being only a series of electrical impulses. However, the object code was an expression of the source code in a form that the computer could read and act upon. It was therefore a translation of a literary work, that is, the source code. The object code was therefore also protected.

---

24. [1988] 2 NZLR 490 (CA), [1989] 3 NZLR 18 (PC). *See also*, *Davies v. TV3 Services Ltd* High Court Auckland CIV-2004-404-1130, 13 Jun. 2005, Williams J.
25. [1989] 2 NZLR 395; (1989) 14 IPR 225.

Subsequently, the Copyright Act 1994 expressly provided that computer software was protected by copyright as a literary work. Under the 1994 Act, the term 'literary work' in section 14 is defined in section 2 as meaning:

> any work, other than a dramatic or musical work, that is written, spoken, or sung; and includes—

(a) a table or compilation; and
(b) a computer program.

Computer programs are therefore now included in the section 2 definition of 'literary work'. Section 2 also provides that 'writing' includes any form of notation or code, whether by hand or otherwise and regardless of the method by which, or medium in or on which, it is recorded; and written has a corresponding meaning. This means that the definition of 'writing' in the Act has now been broadened, so that both source and object code may now be covered. However, there is no definition of 'computer program' in the Copyright Act 1994.

The change to include computer software in the definition of literary work reflects the requirement in the Agreement on Trade Related Aspects of Intellectual Property Rights (TRIPS) Article 10(1), which provides:

> Computer programs, whether in source or object code, shall be protected as literary works under the Berne Convention (1971).

The question of copyright protection for computer software was therefore resolved with the passage of the Copyright Act 1994. The precise scope of copyright protection, and the related question as to what acts constitute infringement, remains uncertain in New Zealand law. Issues remain as to what constitute unprotected ideas as compared to protected expression in relation to copyright law, and also issues as to the extent to which non-literal copying can constitute infringement. There have been relatively few software infringement cases in which these issues were raised. One recent case in which these issues did arise was *Karum Group LLC v. Fisher & Paykel Financial Services Ltd.*[26] This was a case of alleged copyright infringement in relation to a computer program, which raised issues as to the distinction between unprotected ideas and the expression of ideas in the context of computer programs, and the question whether copyright protection extends beyond literal elements to the program's structure, being the programmer's choice of subroutines and relationships and prescribed interactions between them.[27] The Court of Appeal referred to cases from the US[28]

26. [2014] NZCA 389.
27. *Karum Group LLC v. Fisher & Paykel Financial Services Ltd* [2014] NZCA 389.
28. In particular, *Computer Associates International Inc v. Altai* 982 F 2d 693 (2nd Cir 2 1992).

Australia,[29] and the UK,[30] and to the EU Software Directive[31] which, the Court said, provides that the expression of a computer program is protected but ideas and principles underlying any element of a program are not.[32] The Court of Appeal concluded that:[33]

> [W]hile copyright may extend to non-literal elements of a computer program, the scope for protection of such elements is constrained; a plaintiff may not find it easy to distinguish expression from idea, or to establish originality or substantiality, or to prove that the specific elements concerned are not mere functionality or business rules or matters of external necessity.

While the Copyright Act 1994 resolved the question of copyright protection for computer programs, the question of patent protection was left open. There was no statutory exclusion from patentability for computer software in the Patents Act 1953. Computer software was therefore patentable if it met the requirements for patentability under the Act. However, the patenting of software has proved very controversial, with considerable opposition to patentability from the New Zealand software industry, who saw patents for software as a barrier to innovation.

A new Patents Act was passed in 2013, to come into force in 2014. The patenting of computer software proved to be one of the most contentious issues in the course of parliamentary debates on the legislation, and a number of clauses were proposed before the final provision, a new section 11, was agreed. Section 11 of the Patents Act 2013 now provides as follows:

> Computer programs
>
> (1) A computer program is not an invention and not a manner of manufacture for the purposes of this Act.
> (2) Subsection (1) prevents anything from being an invention or a manner of manufacture for the purposes of this Act only to the extent that a claim in a patent or an application relates to a computer program as such.
> (3) A claim in a patent or an application relates to a computer program as such if the actual contribution made by the alleged invention lies solely in it being a computer program.

The effect of this provision is that computer programs 'as such' are excluded from patentability under New Zealand patent law. It does not mean that all computer software is excluded from patentability, and it is likely that a variety of inventions involving

---

29. *Data Access Corp v. Powerflex Services Pty Ltd* [1999] HCA 49.
30. *IBCOS Computers Ltd & Anor v. Barclays Mercantile Highland Finance Ltd & Ors* [1994] FSR 275, *Navitaire Inc v. Easyjet Airline Co Ltd* [2006] RPC 95, *Nova Productions Ltd v. Mazooma Games Ltd & Ors* [2006] EWHC 24, *SAS Institute v. The World Programming Ltd* [2010] EWHC 1829.
31. Directive 1991/250/EEC of 14 May 1991 on the Legal Protection of Computer Programs ('the Software Directive').
32. *Karum Group LLC v. Fisher & Paykel Financial Services Ltd* [2014] NZCA 389, [114].
33. *Karum Group LLC v. Fisher & Paykel Financial Services Ltd* [2014] NZCA 389, [116].

computer software will be patentable under section 11. The use of 'as such' makes this provision similar to the provision in Article 52 of the European Patent Convention, meaning that New Zealand law moves closer to the European approach, with the potential for New Zealand courts to draw on European case law.

Section 11(3) will be significant in interpreting whether a computer program is or is not protectable, as it provides that a claim in a patent or an application relates to a computer program as such if the actual contribution made by the alleged invention lies solely in it being a computer program. Section 11(4) goes on to list factors to be taken into account in determining whether the actual contribution made by the alleged invention lies solely in it being a computer program. Section 11(4) provides:

> (4) The Commissioner or the court (as the case may be) must, in identifying the actual contribution made by the alleged invention, consider the following:

(a) the substance of the claim (rather than its form and the contribution alleged by the applicant) and the actual contribution it makes:
(b) what problem or other issue is to be solved or addressed:
(c) how the relevant product or process solves or addresses the problem or other issue:
(d) the advantages or benefits of solving or addressing the problem or other issue in that manner:
(e) any other matters the Commissioner or the court thinks relevant.

Section 11 provides two examples by way of guidance:

> Examples
>
> A process that may be an invention
>
> A claim in an application provides for a better method of washing clothes when using an existing washing machine. That method is implemented through a computer program on a computer chip that is inserted into the washing machine. The computer program controls the operation of the washing machine. The washing machine is not materially altered in any way to perform the invention.
>
> The Commissioner considers that the actual contribution is a new and improved way of operating a washing machine that gets clothes cleaner and uses less electricity.
>
> While the only thing that is different about the washing machine is the computer program, the actual contribution lies in the way in which the washing machine works (rather than in the computer program per se). The computer program is

only the way in which that new method, with its resulting contribution, is implemented.

The actual contribution does not lie solely in it being a computer program. Accordingly, the claim involves an invention that may be patented (namely, the washing machine when using the new method of washing clothes).

A process that is not an invention

An inventor has developed a process for automatically completing the legal documents necessary to register an entity.

The claimed process involves a computer asking questions of a user. The answers are stored in a database and the information is processed using a computer program to produce the required legal documents, which are then sent to the user.

The hardware used is conventional. The only novel aspect is the computer program.

The Commissioner considers that the actual contribution of the claim lies solely in it being a computer program. The mere execution of a method within a computer does not allow the method to be patented. Accordingly, the process is not an invention for the purposes of the Act.

These examples are helpful, but represent opposite ends of the spectrum. There will be rather more uncertainty at the margins as to whether any particular computer program is patentable. What is clear is that a variety of computer programs will continue to be patentable under the new legislation. This patent protection will be additional to copyright protection.

B. Databases

19. In New Zealand, databases are protected under copyright law. There is no sui generis regime for database protection. New Zealand copyright law protects databases as literary works. Under the Copyright Act 1994, the term 'literary work' in section 14 is defined in section 2 as meaning:

any work, other than a dramatic or musical work, that is written, spoken, or sung; and includes—

(a) a table or compilation; and
(b) a computer program.

Databases are protected as tables or compilations. Section 2 also provides a definition of 'compilation', as follows:

> compilation includes—
>
> (a) a compilation consisting wholly of works or parts of works; and
> (b) a compilation consisting partly of works or parts of works; and
> (c) a compilation of data other than works or parts of works.

The definition of compilation expressly includes compilations of data as well as compilations of works or parts of works. There is therefore no doubt that databases are protected by copyright, so long as they meet the other requirements of protection, including the originality requirement. While the precise requirements for originality in relation to databases remain unresolved in New Zealand, the New Zealand courts have tended to set a low standard for originality. The New Zealand Supreme Court recently considered the question of originality in relation to a compilation case in *Henkel KgaA v. Holdfast New Zealand Ltd.*[34] In that case, the Court said that:

> To be original for copyright purposes the work must originate from its author and must be the product of more than minimal skill and labour… The threshold for originality is a low one and it can be material for other purposes how original the work is; that is, how much skill and labour has gone into its creation. In general terms the greater the originality, the wider will be the scope of the protection which copyright affords and vice versa.

The Supreme Court said that the amount of skill and labour involved had particular relevance in arrangement cases. The skill and labour in the arrangement was what gave the work its originality and if that skill and labour was not great, another arrangement of the same unoriginal underlying features may not have to depart greatly from the copyright arrangement in order to avoid infringement. If the level of originality in the copyright arrangement was low, the amount of originality required to qualify another arrangement of the same elements as original, was also likely to be low. Substantial reproduction of those aspects of the work in which the originality lay must be shown to establish infringement.

It is clear therefore that databases are protected as literary works, being compilations, so long as the selection and arrangement of the data is the product of more than minimal skill and labour, and other statutory requirements are met. Most databases will meet these requirements and receive copyright protection.[35]

Uncertainty remains, however, as to what actions by a defendant will constitute infringement. Database copyright will generally not extend to pre-existing data or

---

34. [2007] 1 NZLR 577(SC), 590.
35. *See also Land Transport Safety Authority of New Zealand v. Glogau* [1999] 1 NZLR 261 (CA), *University of Waikato v. Benchmarking Services Ltd* (2004) 8 NZBLC 101, 561.

facts. Copyright will rather protect the selection and arrangement of that material. The extent of protection will vary with the level of originality of the selection and arrangement. For databases that are of low originality, copyright protection will be relatively thin. Substantial reproduction of the original aspects of the work must be shown to establish infringement. For databases with a higher level of originality, there will be a commensurate higher level of protection against infringement. These principles are clear, but there remains inevitable uncertainty in cases close to the dividing line, and this uncertainty can generally only be resolved by litigation.

C. Others

20. In addition to computer software and databases, a number of other types of work have raised particular legal issues. Categories of work creating particular issues in copyright law include works such as slogans and headlines which raise the question as to whether they qualify as literary works, and the scope of protection to be given to artistic works used in industry. An additional contentious category is the category of works embodying indigenous traditional knowledge in various forms, and these issues are still substantially unresolved. Works embodying traditional knowledge.

21. Aotearoa/New Zealand has a large indigenous Māori population, with strong cultural traditions and a rich body of creative works including a wide variety of artistic works, some very old, some very current. Copyright law is not well suited to the protection of these works. At a simplistic level, many such works do not have a clearly identified author meaning that originality is difficult to establish, and for many the term of copyright will have expired. At a broader level, the protection offered by copyright law does not match the protection required by Māori cultural traditions. In Māori culture, or tikanga, there is a system of rules about how works are made available and used which are not based on the same property conceptions as copyright law.

Māori concerns about the protection of, *inter alia*, Māori artistic and cultural works, were raised in a claim to the Waitangi Tribunal.[36] The Māori intellectual property claim, known as Wai-262, was a claim to Māori cultural and intellectual property, and to indigenous flora and fauna. As addressed by the Tribunal, the Report also encompassed the role of Māori culture, Māori traditional knowledge and Māori identity within Aotearoa/New Zealand. The Waitangi Tribunal reported on the claim in 2011. The Tribunal addressed the claim as its 'first whole-of-government inquiry', and made findings crossing more than twenty government departments and agencies. The Tribunal said that it was for Crown and Māori to negotiate solutions, but the Tribunal recommendations were guidelines for that process.

In relation to Māori artistic and creative works, the Tribunal made a number of specific recommendations. The Tribunal focused on the place in contemporary New Zealand life of core Māori cultural values such as the obligation of Māori groups to act as kaitiaki (cultural guardians) towards taonga (treasured things) such as traditional

36. The Waitangi Tribunal was established by the Treaty of Waitangi Act 1975 as part of the New Zealand judicial system. It acts as a permanent Commission of Inquiry into Maori grievances about Crown breaches of the Treaty of Waitangi. The Treaty of Waitangi was an agreement between the Crown and Maori signed in 1840, and is regarded as a founding document of New Zealand.

knowledge, artistic and cultural works, important places, and significant flora and fauna. The Tribunal distinguished 'taonga works,' where there is an identified kaitiaki (guardian), and 'taonga-derived works', for which there is not, finding that taonga works required strongest protection, and taonga-derived works lesser protection. Taonga works are protected by kaitiaki, who must be enabled to undertake the protection of the work, and the underlying mātauranga Māori (knowledge, wisdom) behind the taonga. The Tribunal said that intellectual property laws are not designed and cannot be the sole means to protect the Māori Treaty interest in taonga works, taonga-derived works, and mātauranga Māori. It recommended a sui generis system which included the following recommendations relating to artistic and cultural works:

- A general objection system whereby anyone can object to derogatory or offensive public use of taonga works, taonga-derived works and mātauranga Māori.
- Establishment of a mechanism whereby kaitiaki can object to and prevent any commercial exploitation of taonga works or closely held mātauranga Māori without appropriate consultation or consent.
- A register of kaitiaki interests, although kaitiaki should have a right to object whether or not they have registered their interest.
- Establishment of an expert commission with multi-disciplinary expertise to administer the objection process, maintain a register of kaitiaki and their mātauranga Māori or taonga works, and publish best practice-guidelines for use, care, protection and custody of taonga works, taonga-derived works, and mātauranga Māori.
- Strengthening of Māori engagement in the processes where Crown enters into international agreements, to identify when such instruments implicate Māori interests, and to ensure appropriate and quality Māori engagement where Māori interests are involved.

The New Zealand government has not yet responded to this report, which has potentially far-reaching implications. New Zealand is also a signatory to the United Nations Declaration on the Rights of Indigenous Peoples 2007, which also creates obligations on the government in relation to indigenous intellectual property rights. In particular, Article 31 provides that:

Article 31

(1) Indigenous peoples have the right to maintain, control, protect and develop their cultural heritage, traditional knowledge and traditional cultural expressions, as well as the manifestations of their sciences, technologies and cultures, including human and genetic resources, seeds, medicines, knowledge of the properties of fauna and flora, oral traditions, literatures, designs, sports and traditional games and visual and performing arts. They also have the right to maintain, control, protect and develop their intellectual property over such cultural heritage, traditional knowledge, and traditional cultural expressions.
(2) In conjunction with indigenous peoples, States shall take effective measures to recognize and protect the exercise of these rights.

We can therefore expect changes in the way New Zealand law protects indigenous works, and it is likely that developments will continue in this area for some time.

§3. Conditions of Protection

I. Formal Requirements

A. Recording Necessary for Some Works

22. Section 15 of the Copyright Act 1994 provides that copyright does not exist in a literary or dramatic or musical work unless and until the work is recorded, in writing or otherwise. Under section 2(1), 'writing' includes any form of notation or code, whether by hand or otherwise and regardless of the method by which, or the medium in or on which it is recorded. For a literary or dramatic or musical work, recording is therefore a prerequisite for protection, and the recording can be in writing or otherwise, meaning that any form of recording technology will be sufficient, so long as the work is recorded. Section 15 also provides that it is immaterial whether the work is recorded by or with the consent of the author.

There is no requirement that artistic works, films, sounds recordings, communication works or typographical arrangements of published editions be recorded.

B. Qualification for Copyright

23. Section 17 of the Copyright Act 1994 sets out the qualifying factors required for copyright to subsist under the Act. Section 17 provides that copyright does not exist in a work unless the requirements of section 18 or section 19 or section 20 are satisfied in respect of that work. A work therefore has to meet the requirements of one of sections 18–20 only.

Section 18 provides that a work qualifies for copyright if the author is, at the material time, a New Zealand citizen, or domiciled or resident in New Zealand, or a body incorporated under the law of New Zealand. Section 18(2) extends these requirements to the equivalent in a prescribed foreign country, or convention country.[37] 'Material time' is defined in section 2, generally it is when the work is made for unpublished works and for published works, when the work is first published.[38] Section 19 provides that, for works other than communication works, a work qualifies for copyright if it is first published in New Zealand or in a prescribed foreign country. Section 20 provides that a communication work qualifies for copyright if it is made from a place in New Zealand or a place in a prescribed foreign country.

---

37. Prescribed foreign countries are listed in the Copyright (Application to Other Countries) Order 1995 (SR 1994/145). These are generally countries signatory to international agreements on copyright. Most countries are included.
38. Copyright Act 1994 s. 2.

II. Substantive Requirements

24. The main substantive requirements are that the work is original, and that it satisfies the other requirements in section 14.

The Copyright Act 1994 sets out the requirements for copyright to subsist. Under section 14, copyright is a property right that exists in original works of one of the specified categories. There is therefore a threshold requirement that a work be original in order to obtain copyright protection. 'Original' is not defined in the Act. However, assistance is provided in section 14(2) which provides that:

(2) A work is not original if—

(a) it is, or to the extent that it is, a copy of another work; or
(b) it infringes the copyright in, or to the extent that it infringes the copyright in, another work.

A work will therefore lack originality if it is, or to the extent that it is, an infringement of copyright in another work. The originality requirement has been interpreted in the cases. Originality is to be assessed in relation to the work as a whole, rather than by dissecting the work and assessing each part.[39] Generally, 'original' means that the work originates from the author, who produced it independently rather than by slavishly copying it from elsewhere. The work need not be new or unique. In producing the work, the author must have expended sufficient skill, labour, knowledge, taste, judgment or capital. The level of skill or labour required is generally quite low, but must not be insubstantial. Whether sufficient skill or labour has been expended will be a question of fact and degree in each case. In *Henkel KgaA v. Holdfast New Zealand Ltd,*[40] the New Zealand Supreme Court said that:

> To be original for copyright purposes the work must originate from its author and must be the product of more than minimal skill and labour… The threshold for originality is a low one and it can be material for other purposes how original the work is; that is, how much skill and labour has gone into its creation. In general terms the greater the originality, the wider will be the scope of the protection which copyright affords and vice versa.

Works based on earlier material may be protected by copyright, so long as sufficient labour and skill are applied to the earlier material. New editions of works, anthologies, compilations and translations may be the subject of copyright. However, where originality is low, the level of protection will also be low, so that it will be harder to prove copying.[41]

The other requirements of section 14 are discussed at §2 Subject Matter of Protection.

---

39. *Ladbroke (Football) Ltd v. William Hill (Football) Ltd* [1964] 1 WLR 273; [1964] 1 All ER 465 (HL).
40. [2007] 1 NZLR 577(SC), 590.
41. *See also Land Transport Safety Authority of New Zealand v. Glogau* [1999] 1 NZLR 261 (CA).

§4. Ownership

I. Section 21

25. Under section 21 of the Copyright Act 1994, generally the person who is the author of a work is the first owner of any copyright in the work. Under section 5, for most works the author is the person who creates the work.[42]

There are important exceptions to the rule that the author is the first owner of the copyright. These exceptions apply where the work is made by an employee in the course of employment, and where a work has been commissioned. Both exceptions are subject to any agreement to the contrary.[43]

26. The first exception is for employee-created works. Section 21(2) provides that where an employee makes, in the course of his or her employment, a literary, dramatic, musical, or artistic work, that person's employer is the first owner of any copyright in the work. Section 2 defines 'employed' as meaning employed under a contract of service or a contract of apprenticeship; and employee, employer and employment have corresponding meanings.

This means that, for the limited range of works covered by section 21(2), if the author is an employee, and makes the work in the course of employment, then the employer is the owner of the copyright.

Determining whether an author is an employee, employed under a contract of service, involves consideration of a number of factors, including the terms of the employment contract, the employer's degree of control, payment and tax arrangements.[44]

Determining whether a work is made in the course of employment is a separate inquiry. The issue arose in the case of *Fleming v. Fletcher Concrete and Infrastructure Ltd*,[45] where the court applied the principles set out in a patent case, *Empress Abalone Ltd v. Langdon*.[46] In *Empress Abalone*, Keith J in the Court of Appeal said that where an employee made an invention in the course of his employment which was part of his duty to make, the law imported into the contract of employment a term that the invention was the property of the employer. The main difficulty was usually that of determining whether the invention concerned was made in the course of the employment, that is, whether it was something that it was the employee's job to invent. In *Fleming*, the Judge applied this approach, and said that the words 'in the course of employment' meant more than 'during the period the employee is employed'. The words meant

42. Under s. 5, the rule differs for computer-generated works, sound recordings, films, communication works and typographical arrangements of published editions.

43. Copyright Act 1994 s. 21(4).

44. *See Stevenson, Jordan and Harrison v. MacDonald and Evans* (1952) 69 RPC 10, *Redrock Holdings Pty ltd v. Hinkley* (2001) 50 IPR 565.

45. *Fleming v. Fletcher Concrete and Infrastructure Ltd* (High Court, Auckland CIV 2005-404-4598, 1 Dec. 2006, Wild J).

46. *Empress Abalone Ltd v. Langdon* [2000] 2 ERNZ 53 (CA).

something more like 'as part of the duties the employee is engaged and instructed to undertake'.[47]

27. The second exception to the rule that an author is the first owner of copyright in a work is the commissioning rule. Section 21(3) provides that:

> Where—
>
> (a) a person commissions, and pays or agrees to pay for, the taking of a photograph or the making of a computer program, painting, drawing, diagram, map, chart, plan, engraving, model, sculpture, film, or sound recording; and
> (b) the work is made in pursuance of that commission,—
>
> that person is the first owner of any copyright in the work.

The commissioning rule was considered in *Pacific Software Technology Ltd and Michael Steele v. Perry Group Ltd and United Gaming Ltd.*[48] In that case, Hammond J in the Court of Appeal said that commissioning is a question of fact. Written agreements are the better practice. In the absence of a written agreement, the law was well settled, as follows:

> First, to 'commission' simply means to 'order' or 'request'.
>
> Second, this commissioning must be antecedent to the work. It must have been arrived at before the work is made.
>
> Third, s 21 requires, in terms, a commission and an agreement to pay. Whilst an antecedent commissioning does not necessarily imply an obligation to pay, usually it will do so. And the very existence of a payment obligation can lend force to the notion of the commission itself. An agreement to pay can be express or implied... For the purposes of a commission there need not necessarily be agreement as to the precise amount to be paid...
>
> Fourth, this payment is a quid pro quo for the copyright: that is, the making of the copyright work, not the physical embodiment of the work itself.
>
> Fifth, the copyright in the commissioned work belongs to the commissioning party so soon as part of it is done. That is, the commission applies to incomplete as well as complete works.

---

47. *Fleming v. Fletcher Concrete and Infrastructure Ltd* (High Court, Auckland CIV 2005-404-4598, 1 Dec. 2006, Wild J) para. [98].
48. [2004] 1 NZLR 164 (CA).

> Sixth, it will be apparent from the foregoing that although it is an agreement of a kind, a commission is closer to a term of art which is employed in the copyright area for the resolution of first ownership issues. To put this another way, the notion of a commission is sui generis to copyright law. It involves the court finding an arrangement of the requisite character between the parties, and what the terms of it are. The very existence of the commission may be inferred.

In a more recent decision, *Oraka Technologies Ltd & Ors v. Geostel Vision Ltd & Ors,*[49] the New Zealand Court of Appeal referred to and applied its decision in *Pacific Software.* Hammond J said that the issue whether there was in law a commissioning of the drawings in that case required a request to make the drawings; an antecedent payment or an agreement to pay for them in money or money's worth, and the making of the drawing.

II. Crown Copyright

28. Crown copyright also involves special ownership rules. The provisions on ownership of copyright in section 21 are, by section 21(5) subject to sections 26 and 28 of the Act. Section 26 relates to Crown copyright, and provides that where a work is made by a person employed or engaged by the Crown under a contract of service, a contract of apprenticeship, or a contract for services, the work qualifies for copyright notwithstanding section 17(1) and the Crown is the first owner of any copyright in the work. This copyright is called Crown copyright. The Crown is defined in section 2 to mean Her Majesty the Queen in Right of New Zealand; and includes a Minister of the Crown, a government department, an Office of Parliament, and the Parliamentary Counsel Office; but does not include a Crown entity; or a state enterprise. In cases of works of joint authorship, the section applies only in relation to those authors employed or engaged by the Crown and the copyright existing by virtue of their contribution to the work.[50]

The Crown copyright provision in section 26 is subject to section 27,[51] which provides that no copyright exists in Bills or Acts of Parliament, regulations, bylaws, the New Zealand Parliamentary Debates, reports of select committees laid before the House of Representatives, judgments of any court or tribunal, reports of Royal commissions, commissions of inquiry, ministerial inquiries, or statutory inquiries or of inquiries established under section 6 of the Inquiries Act 2013. There is no copyright in these works whenever they were made.

Section 28 of the Copyright Act 1994 applies to works made by officers or employees of international organizations, and provides that the international organization will be the first owner of copyright in the work.

---

49. (2010) 88 IPR 227; (2010) 9 NZBLC 103,010; [2010] NZCA 232.
50. Copyright Act 1994 s. 26(4).
51. By s. 26(7) of the Copyright Act 1994.

§5. Transfer

I. Assignment of Copyright

29. Ownership of copyright can be assigned. Moral rights, however, cannot be assigned.[52] Section 113 of the Copyright Act 1994 provides as follows:

113 Transmission of copyright

(1) Copyright is transmissible, as personal or moveable property, by—

(a) assignment; or
(b) testamentary disposition; or
(c) operation of law.

(2) A transmission of copyright may be partial, that is, limited so as to apply—

(a) to 1 or more, but not all, of the things the copyright owner has the exclusive right to do:
(b) to part, but not the whole, of the period for which the copyright is to exist.

Copyright can therefore be assigned in whole or in part. Section 114 provides that 'An assignment of copyright is not effective unless it is in writing signed by or on behalf of the assignor.' No particular form of document is specified. 'Writing' is defined in section 2 to include 'any form of notation or code, whether by hand or otherwise and regardless of the method by which, or medium in or on which, it is recorded'. In *Oraka Technologies Ltd & Anor v. Geostel Vision Ltd & Ors (No. 2)*,[53] the Judge discussed the requirement that assignment must be both in writing and signed by or on behalf of the assignor. He said that the requirements for writing and for a signature are approached broadly, and that it is unnecessary to use the term 'assigned' or any other particular wording so long as the intention is clear. The word 'copyright' need not be expressly used, and no particular form of document is required.[54] E-mail messages, receipts or invoices may be sufficient. Whether or not a document amounted to a valid assignment of copyright depended on the intention of the parties, and very considerable weight would be placed on declarations of the parties' intentions.[55] He said that even where the assets of a business were sold without express reference to copyright, it may

52. Copyright Act 1994 s. 18.
53. High Court, Hamilton, CIV 2005-419-809, 7 Apr. 2011, Allan J.
54. Citing *Lacy v. Toole* (1867) 15 LT 512, *Cray Valley Ltd v. Deltech Europe Ltd* [2003] EWHC (Ch) 728.
55. Citing *Anvil Jewellery Ltd v. Riva Ridge Holdings Ltd* (1987) 1 NZLR 35 (HC); *Messenger v. British Broadcasting Co Ltd* [1927] 2 KB 543, 550; *Seven Network (Operations) Ltd v. TCN Channel 9 Pty Ltd* (2005) 146 FCR 183 (HCA), [36].

be appropriate to imply a term that copyright passed with the goodwill.[56] The Judge said that the validity of an assignment must be determined on an overall consideration of the material, and that if an intention to assign was established and there was evidence in writing signed by the assignor of an intention to assign, that would normally be sufficient. The Court would accept secondary evidence if sufficiently cogent; it was not necessary for the document itself to be produced.

Under section 113, ownership of copyright may be assigned in part only. Partial assignment of copyright may involve assignment of one or more, but not all, of the exclusive rights of the copyright owner as set out in section 16 of the Copyright Act 1994. A copyright owner may therefore assign different rights to different people. Partial assignment may also be for a limited period of time.

Future copyright may also be assigned. Section 116(1) provides that:

> Future copyright shall be capable of being assigned, wholly or partially, in the same manner and in all respects as if the copyright were then in existence, and on coming into existence the copyright shall vest in the assignee or the assignee's successor in title accordingly.

For an assignment of future copyright, the assignment therefore takes effect when the work comes into existence.

II. Licenses

30. Copyright can be licensed. Under section 2, 'copyright license' means a license to do, or authorize the doing of, any restricted act. Restricted acts are listed in section 16. Copyright licenses are not required to be in writing. They can be implied. In some industries, licenses are offered by collecting societies, such as the Australasian Performing Rights Association (APRA) which operates in the music industry.[57] A license can involve all or some of the exclusive rights provided to the copyright owner under section 16. Section 111 of the Copyright Act provides:

(1) A licence granted by a copyright owner is binding on every successor in title to that person's interest in the copyright, except a purchaser in good faith for valuable consideration and without notice (actual or constructive) of the licence or a person deriving title from such a purchaser; and references in this Act to doing anything—

(a) with, or without, the licence of the copyright owner; or
(b) other than pursuant to a copyright licence—
shall be construed accordingly.

---

56. Citing *Greenfield Products Ltd v. Rover-Scott Bonnar Ltd* (1990) 17 IBR 417, 422; *Mono Pumps (New Zealand) Ltd v. Amalgamated Pumps Ltd* [1992] 1 NZLR 728 (HC), 740.
57. *See* http://www.apra.co.nz/ (accessed 8 Dec. 2013).

(2) The licensee under an exclusive licence has the same rights against a successor in title who is bound by the licence as that licensee has against the copyright owner.

Licenses may be exclusive or non-exclusive. 'Exclusive license' is defined in section 2 as meaning:

> a licence in writing, signed by or on behalf of a copyright owner, authorising the licensee, to the exclusion of all other persons (including the copyright owner), to exercise a right that would otherwise be exercisable exclusively by the copyright owner.

Section 123 provides that:

(1) An exclusive licensee has, except against the copyright owner, the same rights and remedies…in respect of matters occurring after the grant of the licence as if the licence were an assignment.
(2) The rights and remedies of the exclusive licensee …are concurrent with those of the copyright owner.

The exclusive licensee therefore has the same rights and remedies as the copyright owner, and holds these rights concurrently with the copyright owner. The exclusive licensee cannot sue the copyright owner for copyright infringement.

§6. Scope of Exclusive Rights

I. Moral Rights

31. The Copyright Act 1994 was the first New Zealand statute to make provision for a system of moral rights in New Zealand copyright law.[58] Moral rights are therefore still relatively new in New Zealand law, and there are relatively few cases as yet.

The New Zealand Court of Appeal has said that:[59]

> The moral rights of authors are provided to enable authors to protect the integrity of their works even though ownership passes to others.

Moral rights are provided for in Part 4 of the Act. The Act provides for the right of attribution, the right to object to derogatory treatment of the work, a right against false attribution and a right of privacy of certain photographs and films. Moral rights cannot be assigned under the Act. However, unlike in some jurisdictions, under section 107 moral rights can be waived by instrument in writing signed by the person waiving the

58. As required by Art. 6*bis* of the Berne Convention for the Protection of Literary and Artistic Works.
59. *Mitre 10 (New Zealand) Ltd v. Benchmark Building Supplies Ltd* [2004] 1 NZLR 26, 34 (CA).

right. A waiver may relate to a specific work, or to works of a specified description, including future works, and must state the rights to which the waiver relates.

The right of attribution, the right to object to derogatory treatment of the work, and the right of privacy of certain photographs and films all expire when the copyright in the work expires. The right against false attribution expires at the end of the period of twenty years from the end of the calendar year in which the person entitled to the right dies.[60]

A. Right of Attribution

32. The right of attribution is in sections 94–97. Section 94 provides that the author of a literary, dramatic, musical, or artistic work has the right to be identified as the author of the work; and that the director of a film has the right to be identified as the director of the work. For literary and dramatic works, it provides that the author of a literary work (other than words intended to be sung or spoken with music) or a dramatic work has the right to be identified as the author of the work whenever the work is published commercially, performed in public, or communicated to the public, or copies of a film or sound recording including the work are issued to the public. The author of a literary work (other than words intended to be sung or spoken with music) or a dramatic work from which an adaptation is made has the right to be identified as the author of the work from which the adaptation is made whenever the adaptation of the work is published commercially, performed in public, or communicated to the public, or copies of a film or sound recording including the work are issued to the public. For musical works, or literary works consisting of words intended to be sung or spoken with music, the author has the right to be identified as the author of the work whenever:

(a) the work is published commercially; or
(b) copies of a sound recording of the work are issued to the public; or
(c) a film whose soundtrack includes the work is shown in public; or
(d) copies of such a film are issued to the public.

A similar right is provided in relation to adaptations.

Authors of artistic works have the right to be identified as the author of the work whenever:

(a) the work is published commercially or exhibited in public; or
(b) a visual image of the work is communicated to the public; or
(c) a film including a visual image of the work is shown in public; or
(d) copies of such a film are issued to the public; or
(e) in the case of a sculpture, a work of architecture in the form of a building or a model for a building, or a work of artistic craftsmanship, copies of a graphic work representing the work, or of a photograph of the work, are issued to the public.

---

60. Copyright Act 1994 s. 106.

For works of architecture in the form of buildings, the author has the right to be identified as such on the building as constructed or, where more than one building is constructed to the design, on the first to be constructed.

Film directors have the right to be identified as the director whenever the film is shown in public or communicated to the public; or copies of the film are issued to the public.

The right to be identified generally means the right to be identified clearly and reasonably prominently in a manner likely to bring the author's identity to the attention of a person seeing or hearing the performance, exhibition, showing, communication work, graphic work or photograph. For buildings, the right is to be identified by appropriate means visible to persons entering or approaching the building. For commercial publications, or in the issue to the public of copies of a film or sound recording, the right is to be identified clearly and reasonably prominently in or on each copy published commercially or issued, or, if this is not appropriate, in some other manner likely to bring the author's identity to the attention of a person acquiring a copy.[61]

The right to be identified must be asserted. The right is not infringed unless the right has been asserted in such a way as to require identification of the author or director. Section 96 provides details of what is required for assertion under the Act. The right may be asserted on an assignment of copyright in the work, by including in the instrument effecting the assignment a statement that the author or director asserts in relation to that work his or her right to be identified as the author or director, or at any time, by instrument in writing signed by the author or director.

There are exceptions to the right to be identified. Section 97 of the Act provides for a number of detailed exceptions to the right to be identified. These exceptions include some of the exceptions to the economic rights in Part 3 of the Act.

B. Right to Object to Derogatory Treatment

33. The right to object to derogatory treatment of a work is provided for in section 98 of the Act. Section 98 provides that the author of a literary, dramatic, musical, or artistic work and the director of a film have the right not to have the work subjected to a derogatory treatment. A 'treatment' of a work means any addition to, deletion from, alteration to, or adaptation of the work, other than a translation of a literary or dramatic work, or an arrangement or transcription of a musical work involving no more than a change of key or register. A treatment is derogatory if, whether by distortion or mutilation of the work or otherwise, the treatment is prejudicial to the honour or reputation of the author or director.[62]

There is very little New Zealand case law on what constitutes derogatory treatment. The interpretation of 'derogatory treatment' was discussed in a recent District Court case, in a strike-out application.[63] The Judge said that the test for derogatory treatment

61. Copyright Act 1994 s. 95.
62. Copyright Act 1994 s. 98(1).
63. *Radford v. Hallensteins Bros Ltd* [2009] DCR 907.

was not yet resolved in New Zealand, and should not rightly be determined on a strike-out application. In relation to treatment, the Judge said that:[64]

> Even reduction in the size, in the context of a reproduction, of a work could amount to treatment of it.[65] Section 98(1)(b)gave examples of 'distortion' and 'mutilation' in the context of a treatment that might be derogatory, but the ensuing 'or otherwise' leaves the field open to interferences not necessarily affecting the work itself.[66]

The Judge also discussed the possible tests for 'derogatory', and the possibility that a 'rational subjectivity' test should apply in New Zealand.[67]

Content of the right to object to derogatory treatment is set out in section 99. The section contains a number of detailed provisions, but generally, the right is infringed by a person who publishes commercially, performs or exhibits in public, or communicates to the public a derogatory treatment or visual image of a derogatory treatment of the work. Issuing to the public copies of a film or sound recording of, or that includes, a derogatory treatment of the work is also covered.[68] The provision also extends to authorizing others to do these acts.[69] The right is also infringed by a person who, in the course of a business, possesses; or sells or lets for hire, or offers or exposes for sale or hire, or exhibits in public or distributes an object that is, and that the person knows or has reason to believe is, a work or a copy of a work that has been subjected to derogatory treatment, and has been, or is likely to be, the subject of any of the acts described as infringing.[70]

There are exceptions to the right to object to derogatory treatment,[71] and particular provisions in relation to films.[72]

C. *False Attribution and False Representation*

34. The moral rights framework also contains a right against false attribution and against false representation.

1. False Attribution

Section 102(2) provides that a person has the right not to have a literary, dramatic, musical or artistic work falsely attributed to him or her as author; and not to have a

---

64. *Radford v. Hallensteins Bros Ltd* [2009] DCR 907, 923.
65. Citing *Tidy v. Trustees of Natural History Museum* (1995) 39 IPR 501.
66. Citing *Morrison v. Leahy Music Ltd and Anor v. Lightbond Ltd* [1993] EMLR 144.
67. *Radford v. Hallensteins Bros Ltd* [2009] DCR 907, 930. On this issue the Judge referred to Ian Eagles, *New Zealand Moral Rights Law: Did Something Get Lost in Translation?* 8 N.Z. Bus. L. Q. 26, 55–56 (2002).
68. Copyright Act 1994 ss. 99(1)–(5).
69. Copyright Act 1994 s. 99(7).
70. Copyright Act 1994 s. 99(6).
71. Copyright Act 1994 s. 100.
72. Copyright Act 1994 s. 101.

film falsely attributed to him or her as director. Section 102(1) provides that the term 'attribution', in relation to a literary, dramatic, musical, or artistic work or a film, means an express or implied statement as to the identity of the author of the work or the director of the film. The right is infringed by a person who issues copies to the public of a work or film in or on which there is a false attribution, or exhibits in public an artistic work or copy of an artistic work in or on which there is a false attribution, knowing or having reason to believe that the attribution is false.[73] Similar provisions apply to performing or showing in public or communicating to the public, where there is knowledge or reason to believe that the attribution is false.[74] The right is also infringed by issuing to the public or public display of material containing a false attribution in connection with any of the acts referred to above.[75]

The right conferred is also infringed by a person who, in the course of a business, possesses a copy of a literary, dramatic, musical or artistic work; or a film in or on which there is a false attribution, or sells or lets for hire, offers or exposes for sale or hire, exhibits in public, or distributes a copy of a literary, dramatic, musical, or artistic work, or a film in or on which there is a false attribution, or in the case of an artistic work, possesses the work when there is a false attribution in or on the work, or sells, or lets for hire, offers or exposes for sale or hire, distributes, or exhibits in public an artistic work in or on which there is a false attribution, knowing, or having reason to believe, that there is such an attribution and that the attribution is false.[76] Authorizing another to do one of the acts in the section is also covered.[77]

2. False Representation

Section 103 provides that a person has the right not to have a literary, dramatic or musical work falsely represented as being an adaptation of a work of which the person is the author. 'Representation' in this context is defined to mean in relation to a literary, dramatic or musical work, 'an express or implied statement as to the work being an adaptation of a work by a particular author'.

False representations of artistic works are also covered, in section 104. Section 104(2) provides that:

> The author of an artistic work has the right not to have the work falsely represented as the unaltered work of the author if the work has been altered after the author parted with possession of the work; and not to have a copy of a work that has been altered after the author parted with possession of the work falsely represented as a copy of an unaltered work of the author; and not to have a copy of an artistic work falsely represented as being a copy made by the author of the artistic work.

Infringing acts for the false representation rights include issuing copies to the public, performing in public, communicating to the public and exhibiting in public. For all of

73. Copyright Act 1994 s. 102(3).
74. Copyright Act 1994 s. 102(4).
75. Copyright Act 1994 s. 102(5).
76. Copyright Act 1994 s. 102(6).
77. Copyright Act 1994 s. 102(7).

these, the person must know or have reason to believe that there is such a representation and that the representation is false.

D. *Right to Privacy of Certain Photographs and Films*

35. The right to privacy in certain photographs and films is not strictly a moral right as internationally understood, but it is included under the Morals Rights header in Part 4 of the Copyright Act 1994. Section 105 applies to people who commission the taking of a photograph or the making of a film for private or domestic purposes, where copyright is owned by some other person, such as the photographer. The person commissioning the work has the right not to have copies of the work issued to the public, or to have the work exhibited or shown in public, or to have the work communicated to the public. The right can be infringed by authorization.[78] There are some limited exceptions to the right.[79]

As noted in relation to copyright ownership, section 21(3) provides that where a person commissions, and pays or agrees to pay for, the taking of a photograph or the making of a film, and the work is made in pursuance of that commission, that person is the first owner of any copyright in the work. This is relevant to the privacy right, as in many cases, unless there is a contract to the contrary, the commissioner of a photograph or film will also own the copyright.

II. Exploitation Rights

36. The exploitation rights in New Zealand copyright law are set out in section 16 of the Copyright Act 1994, which lists the exclusive rights of the copyright owner. Not all of the exclusive rights apply to all categories of copyright works.

A. *Reproduction Right*

37. Under section 16(1)(a) of the Copyright Act 1994, the copyright owner has the exclusive right to copy the work. Section 30 provides that the copying of a work is a restricted act in relation to every description of copyright work.[80] Copying is defined as follows:[81]

copying

(a) means, in relation to any description of work, reproducing, recording, or storing the work in any material form (including any digital format), in any medium and by any means; and
(b) [Repealed]

---

78. Copyright Act 1994 s. 105(4).
79. Copyright Act 1994 s. 105(3).
80. Copyright Act 1994 s. 30.
81. Copyright Act 1994 s. 2.

(c) includes, in relation to an artistic work, the making of a copy in 3 dimensions of a two-dimensional work and the making of a copy in 2 dimensions of a three-dimensional work; and
(d) includes, in relation to a film or communication work, the making of a photograph of the whole or any substantial part of any image forming part of the film or communication work—
and 'copy' and 'copies' have corresponding meanings.

The definition of copying therefore covers copying using any medium or means, and is not linked to any particular technology. Copying includes copying from a two-dimensional work such as a drawing to a three-dimensional work, and vice versa. The definition is broad and flexible.[82]

38. The copyright owner also has the exclusive right to issue copies of a copyright work to the public, whether by sale or otherwise.[83] The issue of copies of a work to the public is a restricted act in relation to every description of copyright work.[84]

'Issue of copies of a work to the public' is defined in section 9 of the Copyright Act to mean the act of putting into circulation copies not previously put into circulation. It does not include the acts of subsequent distribution or sale of those copies, or, except in some cases, the subsequent hiring or loan of those copies, or subsequent importation of those copies into New Zealand, or distribution of imported copies that are not infringing copies (within the meaning as defined in section 12) subsequent to their importation into New Zealand. The copyright owner therefore has a right to prevent others from issuing copies of a work to the public, but the right does not generally extend to cover subsequent distribution. This is the 'first sale' principle.

Different rules, however, apply to the rental to the public of computer programs, where the exclusive rights of the copyright owner include a rental right. Section 9 provides that the issue of copies of a work to the public, in relation to computer programs, includes the rental of copies of computer programs to the public and rental subsequent to those works having been put into circulation. However, this does not include any such rental where the computer program is incorporated into any other thing, and the rental of the computer program is not the principal purpose or one of the principal purposes of the rental, and the computer program cannot readily be copied by the hirer. There is also a special provision extending the right to cover rental of copies of sound recordings and films to the public, including rental subsequent to those works having been put into circulation.

The effect of these provisions is that subsequent distribution or hiring is not generally part of the exclusive right of issuing to the public. This allows for rental and loans by institutions such as libraries. However, subsequent distribution or hiring is part of the right for rental of computer programs (including computer games), sound recordings and films. 'Rental' is defined in the Act, and the definition clearly requires that rental involves payment.[85] There is no definition of 'public' in the Act.

---

82. Infringement by copying is covered under the 'Infringement' heading at §10.
83. Copyright Act 1994 s. 16(1)(b).
84. Copyright Act 1994 s. 31.
85. Copyright Act 1994 s. 2.

B. Performing Right

39. The copyright owner also has the exclusive rights to perform the work in public, to play the work in public, to show the work in public and to communicate the work to the public.

These exclusive rights do not apply to all categories of work. Communicating a work to the public is a restricted act in relation to every description of copyright work.[86] However, the performance of a work in public is a restricted act only in relation to a literary, dramatic or musical work.[87] The playing or showing of a work in public is a restricted act only in relation to a sound recording, film or communication work.[88] This means that the showing of an artistic work in public is not a restricted act, so that acts such as display of works in art galleries and museums do not infringe the right.

There is no definition of 'public', but courts are likely to give weight to the nature of the audience and whether the people in the audience are bound together by a domestic or private tie or by an aspect of their public life.[89]

Where copyright in a work is infringed by the performance, playing, or showing of the work in public by means of apparatus for receiving visual images or sounds conveyed by electronic or other means, the person by whom the visual images or sounds are sent; and the performers shall not be regarded as responsible for the infringement.[90] A person who sends visual images or sounds does not include a person who retransmits visual images or sounds.[91]

For the purposes of this provision, 'performance' is broadly defined, and in general includes any mode of visual or acoustic presentation of a literary, dramatic, musical or artistic work, including presentation of the work by means of a sound recording, film or communication work.[92]

In addition to the performing right in section 16 of the Act, there are specific Performers' Rights provisions in Part 9 of the Copyright Act. These will be discussed below under the heading §9. Neighbouring Rights.

C. Adaptation Right

40. The owner of the copyright in a work has the exclusive right to make an adaptation of the work and to do any of the other restricted acts in relation to an adaptation of the work.[93]

---

86. Copyright Act 1994 s. 33. *See Munhwa Broadcasting Corporation & Ors. v. Young International 2009 Ltd & Anor.* High Court, Auckland, CIV 2010-404-00203, 17 Dec. 2010, Potter J.
87. Copyright Act 1994 s. 32(1).
88. Copyright Act 1994 s. 32(2).
89. *See Australasian Performing Rights Association v. Commonwealth Bank of Australia* (1992) 25 IPR 157, *Australasian Performing Rights Association v. Telstra* (1997) 38 IPR 294 (HCA).
90. Copyright Act 1994 s. 32(3).
91. Copyright Act 1994 s. 32(4).
92. Copyright Act 1994 s. 2. This is a separate definition from that used in relation to performers' rights in the Act.
93. Copyright Act 1994 s. 16.

'Adaptation' is defined in the Act.[94] In relation to a literary or dramatic work, it includes a translation of the work from one language to another, a version of a dramatic work in which it is converted into a literary work or of a literary work in which it is converted into a dramatic work, and a version of the work in which the story or action is conveyed wholly or mainly by means of pictures in a form suitable for reproduction in a book, newspaper, magazine or similar periodical. For computer programs, it includes converting the work from one computer language or code to another. For musical works, it means an arrangement or transcription of the work.

The making of an adaptation of a work is a restricted act only in relation to a literary, dramatic or musical work.[95] An adaptation is made when it is recorded, in writing or otherwise.[96] Doing any of the acts of copying, issuing copies to the public, performing, playing or showing in public or communicating to the public, in relation to an adaptation of a work, is also a restricted act in relation to the literary, dramatic or musical work from which the adaptation was made.[97]

The meaning of 'adaptation' was discussed in *Mitre 10 (New Zealand) Ltd v. Benchmark Building Supplies Ltd*,[98] a comparative advertising case in which the defendant placed stickers on the plaintiff's advertising brochures. The Court of Appeal noted that infringement by adaptation applied only to literary, dramatic or musical works and not to artistic works, so that the Court focussed on the written matter in the brochures which might constitute literary works. The Court held that the use of the brochures did not come within the specific forms of adaptation in the statutory definition. The Court held that:[99]

> Making an adaptation of a work involves producing a different version of the work incorporating the same product of originality of the author but expressing it in a manner which cannot be characterised as copying or reproduction but still presents substantially the same work. Writing a play or film script from a novel, producing object code from a computer program source code, are typical examples…[W]hat matters is that the intellectual content of the original work has been taken.

The Court referred to section 34(2) which provides that an adaptation is made when it is recorded, in writing or otherwise, making it clear that more was involved than merely taking and using the original work without change. The use of the brochures involved no conversion of, or change to, any literary works, but involved only the display of Mitre 10s own reproductions in the form in which they were distributed. There was no infringement by adaptation.

94. Copyright Act 1994 s. 2.
95. Copyright Act 1994 s. 34(1).
96. Copyright Act 1994 s. 34(2).
97. Copyright Act 1994 s. 34(3).
98. [2004] 1 NZLR 26 (CA).
99. *Mitre 10 (New Zealand) Ltd v. Benchmark Building Supplies Ltd* [2004] 1 NZLR 26, 33.

D. *Translation Right*

41. The owner of the copyright in a work has the exclusive right to make an adaptation of the work. 'Adaptation' is defined in the Act as including, in relation to a literary or dramatic work, a translation of the work from one language to another.[100] Translation is therefore covered by the adaptation right as discussed above.

E. *Other Rights*

1. Droit De Suite

42. New Zealand law makes no provision for a *droit de suite* or artist's resale royalty right. A resale royalty right for visual artists has been considered, and in 2007, the then New Zealand government issued a Discussion Paper on the issue.[101] The Discussion Paper considered a resale royalty right and its possible application in a New Zealand context, and offered a number of proposals that could form the basis of a resale royalty right in New Zealand. Submissions were received[102] and the Copyright (Artist Resale Right) Amendment Bill 2008 was drafted.[103] The Bill would have amended the Copyright Act 1994 by inserting a new part to establish a mandatory resale right for artists when their artistic works were resold in New Zealand. However, the Bill was never enacted and was discharged in 2009. There is no current resale royalty right for artists in New Zealand, and no current proposal to implement such a right.

2. Public Lending Right

43. As discussed in relation to the reproduction right, the copyright owner has the exclusive right to issue copies of a copyright work to the public, whether by sale or otherwise.[104] The issue of copies of a work to the public is a restricted act in relation to every description of copyright work.[105] 'Issue of copies of a work to the public' is defined in section 9 of the Copyright Act[106] to mean the act of putting into circulation copies not previously put into circulation. It does not generally include the acts of subsequent distribution or sale of those copies. This 'first sale principle' means that the copyright owner has a right to prevent others from issuing copies of a work to the public, but the right does not generally extend to cover subsequent distribution. The

100. Copyright Act 1994 s. 2.
101. Te Manatu Taonga, Ministry for Culture and heritage, *A Resale Royalty Right for Visual Artists: Options for its Possible Application to New Zealand Discussion Paper*, April 2007, http://www.mch.govt.nz/files/ResaleRoyaltyPublicDiscussionPaper.pdf (accessed 8 Apr. 2014).
102. An analysis of the submissions can be found at http://www.mch.govt.nz/files/resale-royalty-submission-analysis.pdf. (accessed 8 Apr. 2014).
103. The Bill is at http://www.legislation.govt.nz/bill/government/2008/0184/latest/whole.html (accessed 8 Apr. 2014).
104. Copyright Act 1994 s. 16(1)(b).
105. Copyright Act 1994 s. 31.
106. Copyright Act 1994 s. 9.

exceptions, as discussed above, are for the rental to the public of computer programs, sound recordings and films.

The effect of these provisions is that, with the exception of computer programs, sound recordings and films, rental and loan of copyright works by institutions such as libraries is not restricted by copyright. Nationally and internationally, author groups have argued that this ability of libraries to lend copies of works (traditionally the focus has been on books) to the public has led to lost sales and consequentially, lost royalties to authors. Author groups have sought compensation for lost sales revenue resulting from library lending, and this has resulted in public lending right schemes.

In New Zealand, the current scheme was established under the Public Lending Right for New Zealand Authors Act 2008. The purpose of the scheme is stated in section 11 as being 'to provide for New Zealand authors to receive payments in recognition of the fact that their books are available for use in New Zealand libraries'.[107] The scheme provides annual payments to New Zealand authors, who are required to register annually.[108] The scheme only applies to New Zealand authors, defined as New Zealand residents for tax purposes.[109] New Zealand authors are entitled to receive annual compensation based on the number of copies of their works held in New Zealand libraries, which is determined by a survey undertaken by the National Library of New Zealand.[110]

3. Others

44. The owner of the copyright in a work has the exclusive right to authorize another person to do any of the restricted acts in section 16 of the Copyright Act 1994.[111] Authorizing is a restricted act under section 16(1)(i), and is therefore implicitly an infringement under section 29. Under section 16, authorization must occur within New Zealand to be an infringement.

There remains some uncertainty as to the exact interpretation of authorization in New Zealand law, and New Zealand courts have yet to provide a clear direction. The interpretation of authorization was considered by the New Zealand Court of Appeal in *Heinz Wattie's Ltd v. Spantech Pty Ltd.*[112] This was a case in which the plaintiff, Spantech, claimed that in the construction of a potato storage building infringed its copyright, and that the defendant, Heinz Wattie, had authorized the building company to copy Spantech's work. The new building was to be adjacent to existing potato storage buildings constructed by the plaintiff. Heinz Wattie specified in the new building contract that the building was to be 'as per the existing adjacent Potato Stores'. The building company had advised Heinz Wattie that there would be no breach of copyright by its construction. The Court said that Heinz Wattie as the contracting party directed what was to be built through the contractual specifications and accompanying instructions.

107. Public Lending Right for New Zealand Authors Act 2008 s. 11.
108. Public Lending Right for New Zealand Authors Act 2008 s. 13.
109. Public Lending Right for New Zealand Authors Act 2008 s. 7.
110. For details, see the National Library of New Zealand website at http://natlib.govt.nz/publishers-and-authors/public-lending-right-for-new-zealand-authors (accessed 9 Apr. 2014).
111. Copyright Act 1994 16(1)(i).
112. (2005) 11 TCLR 591 (CA).

If following the specifications and instructions necessarily resulted in an infringing copy of Spantech's works, then, in any ordinary sense of the word, the copying having been directed by HW must have been authorized by it.

On the issue of the approach to authorization, the Court said that for authorization, the purported grant of authority must be extant at the date of the act of primary infringement. The Court said that innocence is not a defence to copyright infringement, and that it is normally sufficient if the authorization is an authorization to copy. It does not have to amount to an actual authorization of a breach of copyright. However, the Court made it clear that it was not deciding on the exact extent to which UK,[113] Australian[114] or US decisions applied in New Zealand. It also made no finding on the interaction between authorization and secondary infringement.

§7. Limitations or Exemptions to the Scope of Copyright Protection

45. New Zealand copyright law does not have a general fair use provision, but it does have a substantial number of specific exceptions and limitations. Part 3 of the Copyright Act 1994 provides for permitted acts in relation to copyright works.[115] If an act is a permitted act under these provisions, the doing of the act does not constitute infringement. The provisions of Part 3 are to be construed independently of one another so that the fact that an act is not permitted by one provision does not mean that it is not permitted by another provision.[116]

The following limitations and exemptions are of particular interest.

I. Incidental Copying[117]

46. Section 41 provides that copyright in a work is not infringed by the incidental copying of the work in an artistic work, a sound recording, a film or a communication work. This extends to cover the issuing copies to the public of the work in which the copyright work has been incidentally copied, and playing, showing or communicating the work to the public.[118] For musical works, these must not be regarded as incidentally copied in another work if deliberately copied.[119]

The statute therefore provides that incidental copying in artistic works, sound recordings, films, or a communication works is not copyright infringement. Incidental copying in other categories of work, such as literary, dramatic or musical works, is not covered. The statute does not define 'incidental', and the section has not been considered by New Zealand courts. However, the equivalent provision in the UK

113. *CBS Songs Ltd v. Amstrad Consumer Electronics plc* (1988) 11 IPR 1 (HL).
114. *Moorhouse v. University of New South Wales* [1976] RPC 151 (HCA).
115. Copyright Act 1994 ss 40–93.
116. Copyright Act 1994 s. 40.
117. Copyright Act 1994 s. 41.
118. Copyright Act 1994 s. 41(1).
119. Copyright Act 1994 s. 41(2).

statute has been considered by courts in that country,[120] and has been said to carry its ordinary meaning,[121] and to mean 'not essential, subordinate, merely background'.[122] It is likely that New Zealand courts would take a similar approach. The section can potentially apply to a range of situations, such as showing of pictures or other artistic works as background in a film, or filming an event in which background music is inadvertently recorded.

II. Fair Dealing Defences

47. Sections 42 and 43 contain the 'fair dealing' defences. Section 42 applies to fair dealing with a work for the purposes of criticism, review and news reporting. Fair dealing with a work for the purposes of criticism or review, of that or another work or of a performance of a work, does not infringe copyright in the work if such fair dealing is accompanied by a sufficient acknowledgement.[123] 'Sufficient acknowledgement' means an acknowledgement identifying the work by its title or other description, and the author of the work, unless the author is anonymous or unknown.[124]

Fair dealing with a work (other than a photograph) for the purpose of reporting current events generally does not infringe copyright in the work if such fair dealing is accompanied by a sufficient acknowledgement.[125] However, if the fair dealing for the purpose of reporting current events is by means of a sound recording, film or communication work, it does not infringe copyright in the work and sufficient acknowledgement is not required.[126] In these circumstances, making sufficient acknowledgement may be impractical, but if not, it may assist in a claim of fair dealing. For the provision to apply, the dealing must be 'fair'. In *Television New Zealand Ltd v. Newsmonitor Services Ltd*, the Judge said that:[127]

> A fair dealing is simply a reasonable use. What is reasonable must be judged by looking at the nature of the works themselves and the purpose for which the defendant dealt with them.

The English Court of Appeal considered the meaning of 'fair dealing' for purposes of criticism or review, or reporting current events, in *Pro Sieben v. Carlton*.[128] Robert Walker LJ said that fair dealing was:[129]

120. Section 31 of the Copyright, Designs and Patents Act 1988 has been considered in cases including *Football Association Premier League Ltd v. Panini UK Ltd* [2004] FSR 1 and *Fraser-Woodward Ltd v. BBC* [2005] EMLR 22.
121. *Football Association Premier League Ltd v. Panini UK Ltd* [2004] FSR 1, 14.
122. *Football Association Premier League Ltd v. Panini UK Ltd* [2003] FSR 698, 701-2.
123. Copyright Act 1994 s. 42(1).
124. Copyright Act 1994 s. 2.
125. Copyright Act 1994 s. 42(3).
126. Copyright Act 1994 s. 42(2).
127. [1994] 2 NZLR 91, (1994) 5 NZBLC 103,409; (1993) 27 IPR 441 (HC).
128. *Pro Sieben Media AG v. Carlton UK Television Ltd* [1999] 1 WLR 605, [1999] FSR 610.
129. *Pro Sieben Media AG v. Carlton UK Television Ltd* [1999] 1 WLR 605, [1999] FSR 610. This case was referred to in *Media Works NZ Ltd v. Sky Television Network Ltd* (2007) 74 IPR 205.

> a question of degree...or of fact and impression...The degree to which the challenged use competes with exploitation of copyright by the copyright owner is a very important consideration, but not the only consideration. The extent of the use is also relevant, but its relevance depends very much on the particular circumstances.

Whether any particular dealing is fair is therefore a question of fact and degree. Courts will consider the relevant factors, including the extent of the use and the purpose of the use.[130] In *Sky Network Television Ltd v. Fairfax New Zealand Ltd*,[131] the High Court Judge agreed that fair dealing was a standard whose application can be, and usually is, a question of degree, and that there was always room for argument as to the bounds of the fair dealing obligation.[132] He said that fair dealing is 'a standard and not a rule'.[133]

For section 42 to apply, the use must also be for the purpose of criticism or review, or of reporting current events, as the case may be. The question of purpose in any particular case is one of fact, and courts have emphasized the need to consider the real purpose of the copying in the context of a fair dealing section.[134] Both criticism or review and news reporting are indefinite in scope, and should be interpreted liberally.[135] Criticism or review may be strongly expressed and unbalanced, and is not limited to criticism of style and can extend to the ideas in the work.[136] The purpose of reporting current events is also interpreted liberally,[137] and the events need not necessarily be recent in time if they are a matter of current interest to the public and the material is used properly to report current events.[138] In *Copyright Licensing Ltd v. University of Auckland & Ors*,[139] Salmon J said that it was difficult to think of any circumstances where the reporting of current events would occur other than in some section of the news media.

Section 42 does not provide an exception to copyright infringement for the copying of photographs for the purpose of reporting current events. This provides additional copyright protection to the owners of copyright in photographs.

Section 43 provides an exception to copyright infringement for the purposes of research or private study. It states that fair dealing with a work for the purposes of research or private study does not infringe copyright in the work.[140] In determining whether copying constitutes fair dealing for the purposes of research or private study, a court shall have regard to:[141]

---

130. *See Copyright Licensing Ltd v. University of Auckland & Ors* (2002) 53 IPR 618, *Ashdown v. Telegraph Group Ltd* [2001] EWCA Civ 1142, [2001] 3 WLR 1368, [66]-[71].
131. *Sky Network Television Ltd v. Fairfax New Zealand Ltd* [2016] NZHC 1883.
132. *Sky Network Television Ltd v. Fairfax New Zealand Ltd* [2016] NZHC 1883, [32].
133. *Sky Network Television Ltd v. Fairfax New Zealand Ltd* [2016] NZHC 1883, [44].
134. *See Copyright Licensing Ltd v. University of Auckland & Ors* (2002) 53 IPR 618.
135. *Pro Sieben Media AG v. Carlton UK Television Ltd* [1999] 1 WLR 605, [1999] FSR 610.
136. *Pro Sieben Media AG v. Carlton UK Television Ltd* [1999] 1 WLR 605, [1999] FSR 610.
137. *See Copyright Licensing Ltd v. University of Auckland & Ors* (2002) 53 IPR 618.
138. *Ashdown v. Telegraph Group Ltd* [2001] EWCA Civ 1142, [2001] 3 WLR 1368, [64] (UK CA), *Copyright Licensing Ltd v. University of Auckland & Ors* (2002) 53 IPR 618.
139. (2002) 53 IPR 618.
140. Copyright Act 1994 s. 43(1).
141. Copyright Act 1994 s. 43(3).

(a) the purpose of the copying;
(b) the nature of the work copied;
(c) whether the work could have been obtained within a reasonable time at an ordinary commercial price;
(d) the effect of the copying on the potential market for, or value of, the work; and
(e) where part of a work is copied, the amount and substantiality of the part copied taken in relation to the whole work.

No more than one copy of the same work, or the same part of a work, may be made on any one occasion.[142]

For the section to apply, there must be a fair dealing. This is a similar requirement to the requirement for fair dealing in section 42, but with the important difference that section 43 lists five factors to be considered in determining whether copying constitutes fair dealing for the purposes of research or private study. These five factors are similar to the fair use factors in section 107 of the United States Copyright Act of 1976.[143] These factors do also overlap substantially with the factors considered as relevant by the courts in relation to section 42.

If the fair dealing requirement in section 43 is met, it must be shown that the fair dealing is for the purposes of research or private study. The meaning of 'research or private study' was considered in *Television New Zealand Ltd v. Newsmonitor Services Ltd.*[144] Blanchard J held that research 'involves the study of things, including written materials or those captured in electronic form'. He referred to Beaumont J in *De Garis v. Neville Jeffress Pidler Pty Ltd*[145] who described research as 'a diligent and systematic enquiry or investigation into a subject in order to discover facts or principles'. He noted that 'private' only qualifies the word 'study', and said that 'private study' 'connotes a form of study which is personal to the person undertaking it'. He took the view that a corporation could engage in private study, and that it could even more clearly engage in research with a commercial end in view. He held that the defence 'does not encompass an activity in which the material concerned is simply appropriated and passed on to others for commercial profit of the appropriator'. This interpretation was followed in *Copyright Licensing Ltd v. University of Auckland & Ors.*[146] In that case, in relation to the interpretation of research or private study in section 43, the Judge said that the purpose must be that of the person doing the copying.

III. Transient Reproduction

48. There is an exception from infringement for copying that is transient or incidental and is an integral and essential part of the technological process for making or receiving a communication that does not infringe copyright or enabling the lawful use of, or lawful dealing in the work. The copying must have no independent economic

142. Copyright Act 1994 s. 43(4).
143. 17 U.S.C.A §107.
144. [1994] 2 NZLR 91, (1994) 5 NZBLC 103,409; (1993) 27 IPR 441 (HC).
145. (1990) 18 IPR 292, 298.
146. (2002) 53 IPR 618.

significance.[147] This provision was inserted into the statute in 2008, and there is little case law as yet.[148] It is designed to cover the transient copying associated with the use of digital technologies, particularly internet technologies.

IV. Education, Libraries and Archives

49. There are a number of specific exceptions in the Copyright Act 1994 applying to copying for educational purposes, in sections 44–49. These exceptions are limited in scope, but they do permit some copying, performing, playing or showing of works. Generally, the exceptions apply only to educational establishments as defined.[149]

There are also a number of specific exceptions that apply only to the activities of libraries and archives.[150] These provisions apply to archives and prescribed libraries as defined.[151]

V. Public Administration

50. There are a number of specific exceptions under the broad heading of public administration.[152] Broadly, these are exceptions to facilitate the administration of government. These include copying for parliamentary and judicial proceedings, commissions and statutory inquiries. Some copying by the Parliamentary Library for Members of Parliament is permitted,[153] and there are provisions for Crown use. Acts specifically authorized by statute are also exempted from infringement unless the enactment provides otherwise.[154]

There is no copyright in some categories of work associated with public administration. These include Bills, Acts of Parliament, regulations and bylaws, New Zealand Parliamentary Debates, reports of select committees, judgments and reports of commissions and inquiries.[155]

VI. Exceptions for Particular Categories of Works

51. There are a number of specific exceptions applying to particular categories of work in sections 67–91. The first group of exceptions applies to literary, dramatic, musical or artistic works. Included, among other provisions, is a provision limiting

147. Copyright Act 1994 s. 43A.
148. *See* limited discussion in *Munhwa Broadcasting Corporation & Ors. v. Young International 2009 Ltd & Anor.* (High Court, Auckland, CIV 2010-404-00203, 17 Dec. 2010, Potter J).
149. Copyright Act 1994 s. 2.
150. Copyright Act 1994 ss 50–57A.
151. Copyright Act 1994 s. 50.
152. Copyright Act 1994 ss 58–66.
153. Copyright Act 1994 s. 58.
154. Copyright Act 1994 s. 66.
155. Copyright Act 1994 s. 27.

the duration of copyright for artistic works that have been applied industrially.[156] There is also a provision that permits two-dimensional copying of three-dimensional artistic works on public display.[157] This provision permits the making and selling of drawings, photographs and postcards of works such as buildings and sculptures on public display.[158] There is also an exception for works in expired patents and registered designs. For a literary or artistic work that forms part of an expired patent or design specification that is open for public inspection in the New Zealand Patent Office, copyright in the work will not be infringed if the work is used to make the object.[159]

52. The second group of exceptions relates to computer programs, sound recordings and films. There is an exception allowing for rental of computer programs, sound recordings and films by educational establishments and prescribed libraries, so long as the rental is not for profit and the works have previously been put into circulation.[160] There are also permitted acts in relation to computer programs, including making of back-up copies,[161] decompilation of a program in particular circumstances,[162] and copying or adapting if necessary for lawful use.[163]

There is provision for sound recordings to be played by non-profit organizations in some circumstances.[164] More significant is a 'format-shifting' exception added in 2008 that permits copying of sound recordings for personal use by the owner of the sound recording. The owner must retain ownership of the recoding. No more than one copy may be made for each device for playing sound recordings owned by the owner of the sound recording.[165] The section does not apply if there is a contract to the contrary.[166]

53. The third group of exceptions relates to communication works. The most significant exception in this group, inserted in 2008, allows for recording of communication works for the purposes of time shifting.[167] Section 84 provides that a person (A) does not infringe copyright in a programme included in a communication work if:

(a) A makes the recording solely for A's personal use or the personal use of a member of the household in which A lives or both.
(b) A makes the recording solely for the purpose of viewing or listening to the recording at a more convenient time.
(c) the recording is not made from an on-demand service.
(d) A has lawful access to the communication work at the time of making the recording.

156. Copyright Act 1994 s. 75.
157. Copyright Act 1994 s. 73.
158. *See Radford v. Hallensteins Bros Ltd* (High Court, Auckland, CIV 2006-404-004881, 22 Feb. 2007, Keane J).
159. Copyright Act 1994 s. 74.
160. Copyright Act 1994 s. 79.
161. Copyright Act 1994 s. 80.
162. Copyright Act 1994 s. 80A.
163. Copyright Act 1994 s. 80B.
164. Copyright Act 1994 s. 81.
165. Copyright Act 1994 s. 81A.
166. Copyright Act 1994 s. 81A(2).
167. Copyright Act 1994 s. 84.

However, A does infringe if A retains the recording for any longer than is reasonably necessary for viewing or listening to the recording at a more convenient time.[168] The statute provides the following examples:[169]

> A records a movie to be screened on television because she will be at work when it screens. She watches the movie on the weekend and then later tapes over it. Provided the conditions in s 84(1) are met, the copy that A makes is not an infringing copy.
>
> B copies music from a streamed Internet audio service and keeps the copy as part of B's music collection, in order to listen to it multiple times on demand. Copies made for the home library or collection in this way are infringing copies.

The exception does not apply to on-demand services, but the exact meaning of on-demand services may require judicial interpretation.

Other exceptions relating to communication works include provisions for recording for the purposes of complaining,[170] and incidental recording for purposes of communication.[171] There is also a provision allowing for free public playing or showing of a communication work in limited circumstances.[172] Recording by media monitors is also permitted under specified conditions.[173]

VII. Public Interest Defence

54. One uncertain area of New Zealand copyright law is the scope of any public interest defence to copyright infringement. Section 225(3) of the Copyright Act 1994 provides that nothing in the Copyright Act affects any rule of law preventing or restricting the enforcement of copyright, on grounds of public interest or otherwise. The Act therefore preserves any pre-existing common law defence of public interest.

There are no New Zealand cases that discuss the public interest defence directly. However New Zealand courts are likely to give weight to UK cases. The public interest defence was discussed by the UK Court of Appeal in *Hyde Park Residence Ltd v. Yelland and Others*[174] and in *Ashdown v. Telegraph Group Ltd.*[175] In *Hyde Park,* Aldous LJ said it was not possible to define the circumstances where it was against the policy of the law to use the Court's procedure to enforce copyright. (Mance LJ dissented on

168. Copyright Act 1994 s. 84(2).
169. Copyright Act 1994 s. 84.
170. Copyright Act 1994 s. 83.
171. Copyright Act 1994 s. 85.
172. Copyright Act 1994 s. 87 and s. 87A.
173. Copyright Act 1994 s. 91.
174. [2000] 3 WLR 215, [2000] EMLR 363.
175. [2001] EWCA Civ 1142, [2001] 3 WLR 1368.

this point.) Aldous LJ said that the circumstances must derive from the work in question, not ownership of the copyright. He said that:[176]

> In my view a Court would be entitled to refuse to enforce copyright if the work is:
>
> (i) immoral, scandalous or contrary to family life;
>
> (ii) injurious to public life, public health and safety or the administration of justice;
>
> (iii) incites or encourages others to act in a way referred to in (ii).

The Court of Appeal took a different view in *Ashdown.*[177] Lord Phillips considered the judgment of Aldous LJ in *Hyde Park*, and his treatment of *Lion Laboratories Ltd v. Evans.*[178] Lord Phillips said that the Court did not consider that Aldous LJ was justified in circumscribing the public interest defence to breach of copyright as tightly as he did, and that the reasons for his decision did not depend on the precise scope of the public interest exception identified. Lord Phillips said that the Court preferred the conclusion of Mance LJ in *Hyde Park* that the circumstances in which public interest may override copyright are not capable of precise categorization or definition. The entry into force of the Human Rights Act 1998 (UK) meant that there was the clearest public interest in giving effect to the right of freedom of expression in those rare cases where this right trumps the rights conferred by the Copyright, Designs and Patents Act 1988 (UK). In such circumstances, the Court considered that section 171(3) of the Copyright, Designs and Patents Act 1988 permitted the defence of public interest to be raised. The Court did not consider that this would lead to a flood of cases where freedom of expression is invoked as a defence to breach of copyright. It would be very rare for the public interest to justify the copying of the form of a work to which copyright attaches.

The public interest defence to copyright infringement can potentially apply in any case where there is a public interest sufficient to override the property rights conferred by copyright. One such public interest is the right to freedom of expression. Section 14 of the New Zealand Bill of Rights Act 1990 provides that everyone has the right to freedom of expression, including the freedom to seek, receive, and impart information and opinions of any kind in any form. This right has not been considered by New Zealand courts in relation directly to the public interest to copyright infringement, but it was briefly discussed in relation to copyright in *Television New Zealand Ltd v. Newsmonitor Services Ltd.*[179] In that case, Newsmonitor argued that the Copyright Act

176. *Hyde Park Residence Ltd v. Yelland and Others* [2000] 3 WLR 215, [2000] EMLR 363 [66].
177. *Ashdown v. Telegraph Group Ltd* [2001] EWCA Civ 1142, [2001] 3 WLR 1368 [58]–[59].
178. [1985] QB 526.
179. [1994] 2 NZLR 91, (1994) 5 NZBLC 103,409; (1993) 27 IPR 441 (HC).

1962 (under which the case was decided) should be given a construction consistent with the freedom of expression provision in section 14 of the New Zealand Bill of Rights Act 1990. Blanchard J took a narrow view, and observed that copyright protects not information or ideas but the form in which they are expressed. He held that 'freedom of expression' does not mean freedom to copy the form in which authors have expressed themselves without consent.

Courts have been more willing to let in a public interest defence in relation to access to information in breach of confidence cases.[180] It may be that these arguments will achieve more success in future.

§8. Duration of Protection

55. The general rule on duration of protection for literary, dramatic, musical or artistic works is that copyright expires at the end of the period of fifty years from the end of the calendar year in which the author dies.[181] If the work is computer-generated, copyright expires at the end of the period of fifty years from the end of the calendar year in which the work is made.[182] If the work is of unknown authorship, copyright expires at the end of the period of fifty years from the end of the calendar year in which it is first made available to the public by an authorized act.[183] Works that are covered by Crown copyright are generally protected by copyright for a period of 100 years from the end of the calendar year in which the work is made.[184]

56. There is a special rule for artistic works that are industrially applied. The general rule for artistic and literary works is that copyright expires at the end of the period of fifty years from the end of the calendar year in which the author dies.[185] However, the duration of copyright will be shorter if the artistic work is applied industrially. Section 75 effectively provides that, where an artistic work is applied

180. *See* for example *Attorney-General for the UK v. Wellington Newspapers Ltd* [1988] 1 NZLR 129 (CA). This case pre-dates the New Zealand Bill of Rights Act 1990, but used a similar analysis and found a public interest defence to breach of confidence applied in relation to information about the activities of United Kingdom security services.
181. Copyright Act 1994 s. 22(1).
182. Copyright Act 1994 s. 22(2).
183. Copyright Act 1994 s. 22(3). *See also* s. 22(4).
184. Copyright Act 1994 s. 26(3). For typographical arrangements of published editions, the period is twenty-five years. There are also specific provisions for copyright that vests in certain international organizations, *see* s. 28.
185. Copyright Act 1994 s. 22(1).

industrially as defined,[186] copyright in that work has a shorter duration. Works of artistic craftsmanship applied industrially will have twenty-five years copyright protection. Other artistic works will have sixteen years copyright protection.[187]

57. For sound recordings and films, the rule is that copyright expires at the end of the period of fifty years from the end of the calendar year in which the work is made; or if it is made available to the public by an authorized act before the end of that period, fifty years from the end of the calendar year in which it is made available, whichever is the later.[188] The rule for communication works is similar. Copyright in a communication work expires at the end of the period of fifty years from the end of the calendar year in which the communication work is first communicated to the public.[189] Copyright in a typographical arrangement of a published edition expires at the end of the period of twenty-five years from the end of the calendar year in which the edition is first published.[190]

Note that for works created before commencement of the Copyright Act 1994, provisions of the Copyright Act 1962 may apply in respect of duration of copyright.

58. For moral rights, duration provisions are in section 106 of the Copyright Act 1994. The right to be identified,[191] the right to object to derogatory treatment[192] and the privacy right for photographs and films,[193] have the same duration as the economic rights in the work.[194] The false attribution and false representation rights,[195] expire at the end of the period of twenty years from the end of the calendar year in which the person who is entitled to the right dies.[196]

---

186. Copyright Act 1994 s. 75(4) and (5) provide:
- For the purposes of subsection (1), an artistic work is applied industrially if:
a. more than 50 copies in 3 dimensions are made of the work, for the purposes of sale or hire; or
b. the work is copied in 3 dimensions in 1 or more objects manufactured in lengths, for the purposes of sale or hire; or
c. the work is copied as a plate that has been used to produce:
- more than 50 copies of an object in 3 dimensions for the purpose of sale or hire; or
- 1 or more objects in 3 dimensions manufactured in lengths for the purposes of sale or hire.
- For the purposes of subsection (4), 2 or more copies in 3 dimensions that are of the same general character and intended for use together are a single copy.

187. The section does not apply to sculptures that are not a cast or pattern for an object that has a primarily utilitarian function; or works of architecture, being a buildings or a model for a building. *See* Copyright Act 1994 s. 75(2).
188. Copyright Act 1994 s. 23. *See* s. 23(2) for interpretation of 'made available to the public'.
189. Copyright Act 1994 s. 24.
190. Copyright Act 1994 s. 25.
191. Copyright Act 1994 s. 94.
192. Copyright Act 1994 s. 98.
193. Copyright Act 1994 s. 105.
194. Copyright Act 1994 s. 106(1).
195. Copyright Act 1994 ss 102–104.
196. Copyright Act 1994 s. 106(2).

§9. Neighbouring Rights

59. The New Zealand Copyright Act does not make clear distinctions between copyright and neighbouring rights. Section 14 provides that copyright is a property right that exists in original works of the following descriptions:

(a) literary, dramatic, musical or artistic works;
(b) sound recordings;
(c) films;
(d) communication works;
(e) typographical arrangements of published editions.

These latter categories, sound recordings, films, communication works and typographical arrangements can be described as neighbouring rights, but are generally treated as categories of copyright works under the statute. There are some particular rules applying to these works, for example as to duration of protection.[197]

60. Performers' rights are provided for in Part 9 of the Copyright Act. Four rights are provided to performers. Sections 171–174 provide that a performer's rights are infringed by a person who, without the performer's consent:

- makes, otherwise than for his or her private and domestic use, a recording of the whole or any substantial part of a performance; or communicates live to the public the whole or any substantial part of a performance;[198]
- by means of a recording, shows in public, plays in public, or communicates to the public the whole or a substantial part of a performance. This applies where the recording was made without the performer's consent; and the person knew or had reason to believe that the recording was made without the performer's consent;[199]
  otherwise than for that person's private and domestic use, copies a recording if the person knows or has reason to believe that the recording was made without the performer's consent.[200] This also applies where the copy is made for purposes other than those to which the performer has consented, or other than those for which exemptions apply;[201]
- imports into New Zealand otherwise than for that person's private and domestic use; or in the course of a business, possesses, sells, lets for hire, offers or exposes

197. Copyright Act 1994 ss 23–25.
198. Copyright Act 1994 s. 171. Note that under s. 171(2), damages shall not be awarded against a defendant who shows that at the time of the infringement the defendant believed on reasonable grounds that the performer's consent had been given.
199. Copyright Act 1994 s. 172.
200. Copyright Act 1994 s. 173(1).
201. Copyright Act 1994 s. 173(3). Note that under s. 173(2) and (4), damages shall not be awarded against a defendant who shows that at the time of the infringement the defendant believed on reasonable grounds that the performer's consent to the recording or copying of the recording had been given.

for sale or hire, or distributes a recording that is, and that the person knows or has reason to believe is, an illicit recording.[202]

Performers' rights in a performance last until the end of the period of fifty years from the end of the calendar year in which the performance takes place.[203] The rights are not assignable but can be transmitted on death.[204]

These rights provide some protection for performers and performances. There is a separate definition of 'performance'.[205] The definition is quite broad, covering dramatic and musical performances, variety acts and readings or recitations. A performance is a live performance given in New Zealand or in a convention country,[206] or given by a New Zealand citizen or New Zealand resident in any country. However, there are some significant exclusions. Sporting performances are expressly excluded. Reading, recitals or delivery of news and information is also excluded.

There are a number of permitted acts in relation to performers' rights. These include incidental copying,[207] transient reproduction,[208] and a defence of fair dealing for the purposes of criticism, review or reporting current events.[209] There are also a number of education exceptions.[210]

Performers' rights in New Zealand are relatively limited. New Zealand is not a party to the WIPO Performances and Phonograms Treaty, although consideration was given to this as part of a reform process commencing in 2001.[211]

§10. Infringement and Remedies

61. In New Zealand law, there is a distinction between primary infringement, which is strict liability with no knowledge requirement, and secondary infringement in which there is a knowledge requirement.

202. Copyright Act 1994 s. 174.
203. Copyright Act 1994 s. 193.
204. Copyright Act 1994 s. 194.
205. Copyright Act 1994 s. 169.
206. A convention country is an entity that is a party to an international agreement or arrangement relating to performers' rights. Copyright Act 1994 s. 169.
207. Copyright Act 1994 s. 175.
208. Copyright Act 1994 s. 175A.
209. Copyright Act 1994 s. 176.
210. Copyright Act 1994 ss 177–179.
211. Ministry of Economic Development, *Performers' Rights: A Discussion Paper*, July 2001, http://www.med.govt.nz/business/intellectual-property/pdf-docs-library/copyright/performers-rights-discussion-paper-pdf (accessed 9 Apr. 2014).

I. Primary Infringement

62. In New Zealand law, copyright is infringed by a person who, other than pursuant to a copyright license,[212] does any restricted act. Restricted acts are listed in section 16. Section 16 provides that the owner of the copyright in a work has the exclusive right to do the following acts in New Zealand:

(a) to copy the work;
(b) to issue copies of the work to the public, whether by sale or otherwise;
(c) to perform the work in public;
(d) to play the work in public;
(e) to show the work in public;
(f) to communicate the work to the public;
(g) to make an adaptation of the work;
(h) to do any of the acts referred to in any of paragraphs (a)–(f) in relation to an adaptation of the work;
(i) to authorize another person to do any of the acts referred to in any of paragraphs (a)–(h).

If another person does one of these restricted acts in relation to a work without the copyright owner's consent, that person is infringing copyright. Sections 30–34 also provide that each restricted act is an infringement. This covers copying, issuing copies to the public, performing, playing, showing the work in public, communicating a work to the public, making an adaptation or doing any of the above in relation to an adaptation. (Adaptation is separately defined in section 2). Infringement also includes authorizing any person to do a restricted act by section 16(1)(i).

Section 29(2) also provides that the doing of a restricted act can be in relation to the work as a whole or any substantial part of it, and either direct or indirect. It is immaterial whether any intervening acts themselves infringe copyright. The infringement provisions are subject to the exceptions and limitations as discussed.

A. Infringement by Copying

63. The most common head of primary infringement is infringement by copying. As defined, 'copying' means reproducing, recording, or storing the work in any material form (including any digital format), in any medium and by any means, and includes, in relation to an artistic work, the making of a copy in three dimensions of a two-dimensional work and the making of a copy in two dimensions of a three-dimensional work, and includes, in relation to a film or communication work, the making of a photograph of the whole or any substantial part of any image forming part of the film or communication work.[213] Section 30 provides that the copying of a work is a restricted act in relation to every description of copyright work. Under section 29, copying can be of the whole work or a substantial part of the work, and can be direct or indirect.

212. The Copyright Act 1994 s. 2 provides that 'copyright license' means a license to do, or authorize the doing of, any restricted act.
213. Copyright Act 1994 s. 2.

In *Wham-O Manufacturing Co v. Lincoln Industries Ltd*,[214] the Court of Appeal set out the requirements for infringement by reproduction:

(a) The reproduction must be either of the entire work or of a substantial part.
(b) There must be sufficient objective similarity between the infringing work and the copyright work, or a substantial part thereof.
(c) There must be some causal connection between the copyright work and the infringing work. The copyright must be the source from which the infringing work is derived.

In determining an infringement action, a court will therefore consider whether there is objective similarity and causal connection and whether a substantial part has been taken.

64. Objective similarity and causal connection: In *Francis Day Hunter v. Bron*[215] Upjohn J said that the first issue, as to whether there is sufficient objective similarity to draw an inference of copying, is an objective question of fact. The second issue of causal connection is whether the defendant copied the plaintiff's work or produced an independent work. This is a subjective question, and also a question of fact. The degree of similarity is important in reaching this subjective conclusion.

In *Henkel KgaA v. Holdfast New Zealand Ltd*,[216] the New Zealand Supreme Court considered copyright infringement in the context of an allegation of indirect infringement of copyright in a design drawing for packaging. In relation to copying, the Supreme Court said:[217]

> The ultimate issue in a breach of copyright case concerns derivation not similarity, albeit the degree of similarity between the copyright work and the allegedly infringing work has evidentiary significance. Proof of copying will seldom be direct; in most cases the court will rely on inference. The closer the similarity between the two works the stronger the inference is likely to be that the one was copied from the other. If the alleged infringer has had access to, and therefore an opportunity to copy, the copyright work, and the similarity between the works supports an inference of copying, it may well be appropriate for the court to conclude, on the balance of probabilities, that there was indeed copying. This of course is subject always to the evaluation of any evidence there may be that no copying actually took place.

In assessing similarity, courts will focus on the similarities rather than the differences.[218]

65. Substantial part: Generally, the courts assess substantial part by looking at the quality of what has been taken rather than the quantity. It is a matter of fact and

214. [1984] 1 NZLR 641 (CA).
215. [1963] Ch 587.
216. [2007] 1 NZLR 577(SC).
217. *Henkel KgaA v. Holdfast New Zealand Ltd* [2007] 1 NZLR 577, 592(SC).
218. *Bleiman v. News Media (Auckland) Ltd* [1994] 2 NZLR 673, 679, *Thornton Hall Manufacturing Ltd v. Shanton Apparel Ltd* (No 2) [1989] 1 NZLR 239, 246–247, *Designers Guild Ltd v. Russell Williams (Textiles) Ltd* [2001] 1 All ER 700, 708–709.

degree in each case. The issue of substantial part was considered by the House of Lords in *Ladbroke (Football) Ltd v. William Hill (Football) Ltd.*[219] Lord Reid said that whether a substantial part has been copied depends much more on the quality than on the quantity of what he has taken. He said that:[220]

> One test may be whether the part which he has taken is novel or striking, or is merely a commonplace arrangement of ordinary words or well-known data. So it may sometimes be a convenient short cut to ask whether the part taken could by itself be the subject of copyright. But, in my view, that is only a short cut, and the more correct approach is first to determine whether the plaintiff's work as a whole is 'original' and protected by copyright, and then to inquire whether the part taken by the defendant is substantial.

He said that dissecting the plaintiff's work and asking whether each section could be protected by copyright by itself can produce a wrong result, and the whole work may be copyright even if parts are not. Lord Pearce also said that whether a part is substantial depends on its quality rather than its quantity. Reproduction of a part which by itself is not original will not normally be a substantial part of the copyright and therefore will not be protected.

New Zealand courts have adopted and followed the *Ladbroke* approach.[221] New Zealand courts have also referred to the test as being 'whether the essence of the copyright work has been taken'.[222] The degree of originality may be relevant, the less original the work, the less likely that substantial part will be found to be copied.[223] The issue of substantiality was recently considered by the New Zealand Supreme Court in *Henkel KgaA v. Holdfast New Zealand Ltd.*[224] In relation to substantial part, the Supreme Court said that:

> It is not necessary for the plaintiff to show that the defendant copied the whole of the copyright work or that the copying was exact. It is enough if the plaintiff demonstrates that the defendant copied a substantial part of the copyright work. This can sometimes be a difficult matter of evaluation and is usually the most difficult question which arises in copyright cases. What amounts to a substantial part in an artistic work case depends more on qualitative visual impression rather than on quantitative analysis. As it has helpfully been put, what must have been copied is the essence of the copyright work. This is a subject upon which, in borderline cases, minds can reasonably differ and it is appropriate for appellate courts to give to the trial judge's assessment the degree of latitude that conventionally applies to appellate review of a discretion.

---

219. [1964] 1 All ER 465 (HL).
220. *Ladbroke (Football) Ltd v. William Hill (Football) Ltd* [1964] 1 All ER 465, 469.
221. *See* for example *Bleiman v. News Media (Auckland) Ltd* [1994] 2 NZLR 673, 678, *see also Henkel KgaA v. Holdfast New Zealand Ltd* [2007] 1 NZLR 577, 592.
222. *Bleiman v. News Media (Auckland) Ltd* [1994] 2 NZLR 673, 678.
223. *Karum Group LLC v. Fisher & Paykel Financial Services Ltd* [2014] NZCA 389, [88]. *See also Henkel KgaA v. Holdfast New Zealand Ltd* [2007] 1 NZLR 577, [41].
224. [2007] 1 NZLR 577, 592.

Under section 29(2), copying can be direct or indirect, and it is immaterial whether any intervening acts themselves infringe copyright. In relation to copying, direct infringement means copying a plaintiff's copyright work. By contrast, indirect infringement may occur where the defendant copies something which is itself a reproduction of the plaintiff's copyright work. The copy must still be of the whole or a substantial part of the plaintiff's work, but the copying can be indirect. The Copyright Act 1994 section 2 definition of 'copying' explicitly includes two-dimensional to three-dimensional copying and vice versa.

In New Zealand copyright law, industrial design drawings and models have copyright protection as artistic works. Indirect copying is common in commercial design cases, for example where copyright in a drawing is indirectly infringed by copying the object that is produced from the drawing. Typically, the copyright works involved in these cases will be drawings or models, but the defendant will have copied the product itself, likely without access to drawings or models. The copying of the product will then indirectly infringe copyright in the drawings and/or models. An example is the case of *Thornton Hall Manufacturing Ltd v. Shanton Apparel Ltd* where copyright in drawings and model for a dress design was infringed by copying the dress.[225]

Section 29(2) provides that it is immaterial whether any intervening acts themselves infringe copyright. This provision confirms the decision in *Frank M Winstone (Merchants) Ltd v. Plix Products Ltd.*[226] In that case, the defendant had designed kiwifruit packaging using the New Zealand Kiwifruit Authority's Specifications and New Zealand Kiwifruit Exporters Association's Instructions. The designer was told not to look at, and never saw, the plaintiff's products or drawings. However, the specifications and instructions were based on the plaintiff's product designs. The results of the defendant's design process were very similar to the plaintiff's products, because they were based on specifications which in turn were based on the plaintiff's designs. The Court held that the plaintiff's copyright had been indirectly infringed. The intervening acts of the Authority and Association did not prevent a finding of infringement. Cooke J said that in principle a reproduction may be the result of indirect copying. He said that:[227]

> The question must always be whether the work alleged to be an infringement can fairly be said to be a reproduction of the copyright work or of a substantial part of that work. If words alone enable a drawing to be reproduced, it seems to us that copyright in the drawing can be infringed. It would be dangerous to hold otherwise. And if words alone were capable of enabling a copyright painting to be reproduced, we see insufficient reason for a different conclusion.

The provision in section 29(2)(b) that it is immaterial whether any intervening acts themselves infringe copyright was inserted into the new Act confirming the approach taken by the Court of Appeal in *Plix*.

225. *Thornton Hall Manufacturing Ltd v. Shanton Apparel Ltd* (No 2) [1989] 1 NZLR 239. *Henkel KgaA v. Holdfast New Zealand Ltd* [2007] 1 NZLR 577, a case about drawings for packaging, is another example.
226. [1985] 1 NZLR 376, (1985) 5 IPR 156 (CA).
227. *Frank M Winstone(Merchants) Ltd v. Plix Products Ltd* [1985] 1 NZLR 376, 380.

B. *Infringement by Issuing Copies to the Public*

66. The copyright owner has the exclusive right to issue copies of a copyright work to the public, whether by sale or otherwise.[228] The issue of copies of a work to the public is a restricted act in relation to every description of copyright work.[229] It is therefore an infringement under section 29 for a person to issue copies of a copyright work to the public without the consent of the copyright owner. This applies to the whole work or to a substantial part of the work.[230] There is no definition of 'public' in the Act.

'Issue of copies of a work to the public' is defined in section 9 of the Copyright Act to mean the act of putting into circulation copies not previously put into circulation. It does not include the acts of subsequent distribution or sale of those copies, or, except in some cases, the subsequent hiring or loan of those copies, or subsequent importation of those copies into New Zealand, or distribution of imported copies that are not infringing copies (within the meaning as defined in section 12) subsequent to their importation into New Zealand. The copyright owner therefore has a right to prevent others from issuing copies of a work to the public, but the right does not generally extend to cover subsequent distribution. This is the 'first sale' principle.

However, different rules apply to the rental to the public of computer programs, where the exclusive rights of the copyright owner include a rental right. Section 9 provides that the issue of copies of a work to the public, in relation to computer programs, includes the rental of copies of computer programs to the public and rental subsequent to those works having been put into circulation. This does not include any such rental where the computer program is incorporated into any other thing; and the rental of the computer program is not the principal purpose or one of the principal purposes of the rental, and the computer program cannot readily be copied by the hirer. There is also a special provision extending the right to cover rental of copies of sound recordings and films to the public, including rental subsequent to those works having been put into circulation. 'Rental' is defined in the Act, and the definition clearly requires that rental involves payment.[231]

C. *Infringement by Performance or Playing or Showing in Public*

67. The copyright owner also has the exclusive rights to perform the work in public, to play the work in public, to show the work in public and to communicate the work to the public. The performance of a work in public is a restricted act only in relation to a literary, dramatic or musical work.[232] The playing or showing of a work in public is a restricted act only in relation to a sound recording, film or communication work.[233] It is an infringement under section 29 for a person to do any of these restricted acts in relation to a work in the category in relation to which the act is restricted,

228. Copyright Act 1994 s. 16(1)(b).
229. Copyright Act 1994 s. 31.
230. Copyright Act 1994 s. 29(2).
231. Copyright Act 1994 s. 2.
232. Copyright Act 1994 s. 32(1).
233. Copyright Act 1994 s. 32(2).

without the consent of the copyright owner. Doing an act that is not restricted for that category of work will not constitute infringement. For example, the showing of an artistic work in public is not a restricted act, so that acts such as display of works in art galleries and museums do not infringe the right. Infringement can be in relation to the whole work or to a substantial part.[234]

There is no definition of 'public', but courts are likely to give weight to the nature of the audience and whether the people in the audience are bound together by a domestic or private tie or by an aspect of their public life.[235]

Where copyright in a work is infringed by the performance, playing or showing of the work in public by means of apparatus for receiving visual images or sounds conveyed by electronic or other means, the person by whom the visual images or sounds are sent; and the performers shall not be regarded as responsible for the infringement.[236] A person who sends visual images or sounds does not include a person who retransmits visual images or sounds.[237]

For the purposes of this provision, 'performance' is broadly defined, and in general includes any mode of visual or acoustic presentation of a literary, dramatic, musical or artistic work, including presentation of the work by means of a sound recording, film or communication work.[238]

D. *Infringement by Communicating to the Public*

68. Communicating a work to the public is a restricted act in relation to every description of copyright work.[239] Copyright is infringed by any person who communicates a work, or a substantial part of work, to the public, without a license from the copyright owner.[240] Section 2 provides that 'communicate' means to transmit or make available by means of a communication technology, including by means of a telecommunications system or electronic retrieval system.

E. *Infringement by Making an Adaptation or by an Act Done in Relation to an Adaptation*

69. The owner of the copyright in a work has the exclusive right to make an adaptation of the work and to do any of the other restricted acts in relation to an adaptation of the work.[241] The making of an adaptation of a work is a restricted act only in relation to a literary, dramatic or musical work.[242] It is therefore an infringement

234. Copyright Act 1994 s. 29(2).
235. *See Australasian Performing Rights Association v. Commonwealth Bank of Australia* (1992) 25 IPR 157, *Australasian Performing Rights Association v. Telstra* (1997) 38 IPR 294 (HCA).
236. Copyright Act 1994 s. 32(3).
237. Copyright Act 1994 s. 32(4).
238. Copyright Act 1994 s. 2. This is a separate definition from that used in relation to performers' rights in the Act.
239. Copyright Act 1994 s. 33. *See Munhwa Broadcasting Corporation & Ors. v. Young International 2009 Ltd & Anor.* High Court, Auckland, CIV 2010-404-00203, 17 Dec. 2010, Potter J.
240. Copyright Act 1994 s. 29.
241. Copyright Act 1994 s. 16.
242. Copyright Act 1994 s. 34(1).

to make an adaptation of a work or a substantial part of a work to which the adaptation right applies, otherwise than with the consent of the copyright owner.[243]

An adaptation is made when it is recorded, in writing or otherwise.[244] Doing any of the acts of copying, issuing copies to the public, performing, playing or showing in public or communicating to the public, in relation to an adaptation of a work, is also a restricted act in relation to the literary, dramatic, or musical work from which the adaptation was made.[245] These acts will also constitute infringement if done without a license from the copyright owner.[246]

'Adaptation' is defined in the Act.[247] In relation to a literary or dramatic work, it includes a translation of the work from one language to another, a version of a dramatic work in which it is converted into a literary work or of a literary work in which it is converted into a dramatic work, and a version of the work in which the story or action is conveyed wholly or mainly by means of pictures in a form suitable for reproduction in a book, newspaper, magazine or similar periodical. For computer programs, it includes converting the work from one computer language or code to another. For musical works, it means an arrangement or transcription of the work.

The meaning of 'adaptation' was discussed in *Mitre 10 (New Zealand) Ltd v. Benchmark Building Supplies Ltd*[248] a comparative advertising case in which the defendant placed stickers on the plaintiff's advertising brochures. The Court of Appeal noted that infringement by adaptation applied only to literary, dramatic or musical works and not to artistic works, so that the Court focussed on the written matter in the brochures which might constitute literary works. The Court held that the use of the brochures did not come within the specific forms of adaptation in the statutory definition. The Court held that:

> Making an adaptation of a work involves producing a different version of the work incorporating the same product of originality of the author but expressing it in a manner which cannot be characterised as copying or reproduction but still presents substantially the same work. Writing a play or film script from a novel, producing object code from a computer program source code, are typical examples…[W]hat matters is that the intellectual content of the original work has been taken.

The Court referred to section 34(2) which provides that an adaptation is made when it is recorded, in writing or otherwise, making it clear that more was involved than merely taking and using the original work without change. The use of the brochures involved no conversion of, or change to, any literary works, but involved only the display of Mitre 10s own reproductions in the form in which they were distributed. There was no infringement by adaptation.

243. Copyright Act 1994 s. 29.
244. Copyright Act 1994 s. 34(2).
245. Copyright Act 1994 s. 34(3).
246. Copyright Act 1994 s. 29.
247. Copyright Act 1994 s. 2.
248. [2004] 1 NZLR 26 (CA).

F. Infringement by Authorization

70. The owner of the copyright in a work has the exclusive right to authorize another person to do any of the restricted acts in section 16 of the Copyright Act 1994.[249] Authorizing is a restricted act under section 16(1)(i), and is therefore implicitly an infringement under section 29. Under section 16, authorization must occur within New Zealand to be an infringement. It is an infringement to authorize another person to do any of the restricted acts in relation to any category of work without a license from the copyright owner. The authorization can relate to the whole work or to a substantial part of the work.[250]

There remains some uncertainty as to the exact interpretation of authorization in New Zealand law, and New Zealand courts have yet to provide a clear direction. The interpretation of authorization was considered by the New Zealand Court of Appeal in *Heinz Wattie's Ltd v. Spantech Pty Ltd.*[251] This was a case in which the plaintiff, Spantech, claimed that in the construction of a potato storage building infringed its copyright, and that the defendant, Heinz Wattie, had authorized the building company to copy Spantech's work. The new building was to be adjacent to existing potato storage buildings constructed by the plaintiff. Heinz Wattie specified in the new building contract that the building was to be 'as per the existing adjacent Potato Stores'. The building company had advised Heinz Wattie that there would be no breach of copyright by its construction. The Court said that Heinz Wattie as the contracting party directed what was to be built through the contractual specifications and accompanying instructions. If following the specifications and instructions necessarily resulted in an infringing copy of Spantech's works, then, in any ordinary sense of the word, the copying having been directed by HW must have been authorized by it.

On the issue of the approach to authorization, the Court said that for authorization, the purported grant of authority must be extant at the date of the act of primary infringement. The Court said that innocence is not a defence to copyright infringement, and that it is normally sufficient if the authorization is an authorization to copy. It does not have to amount to an actual authorization of a breach of copyright. However, the Court made it clear that it was not deciding on the exact extent to which UK,[252] Australian[253] or US decisions applied in New Zealand. It also made no finding on the interaction between authorization and secondary infringement.

II. Secondary Infringement

71. There are provisions in the Copyright Act 1994 for secondary infringement, which differs from primary infringement in that there is a requirement for knowledge in the sense of actual knowledge or reason to believe.

249. Copyright Act 1994 16(1)(i).
250. Copyright Act 1994 s. 29.
251. (2005) 11 TCLR 591 (CA).
252. *CBS Songs Ltd v. Amstrad Consumer Electronics plc* (1988) 11 IPR 1 (HL).
253. *Moorhouse v. University of New South Wales* [1976] RPC 151 (HCA).

A. Infringement by Importation

72. Section 35 provides that it is generally an infringement of copyright in a work to import into New Zealand without a copyright license an object that is an infringing copy of the work where the person importing the infringing copy knows or has reason to believe that the object is an infringing copy.[254] The section only applies if the object was imported into New Zealand other than for the importing person's private and domestic use. The section has some exceptions to permit parallel importing.[255]

Infringing copy is defined in section 12. Generally, an object is an infringing copy if its making constitutes an infringement of the copyright in the work in question. An object that a person imports, or proposes to import, into New Zealand is an infringing copy if the making of the object constituted an infringement of the copyright in the work in question in the country in which the object was made, or the importer would have infringed the copyright in the work in question in New Zealand, had the importer made the object in New Zealand.

There are special provisions applying to importation of sound recordings, films or computer programs.[256]

B. Infringement by Possessing or Dealing with an Infringing Copy

73. It is a secondary infringement of copyright to possess or deal with an infringing copy. Section 36 provides that copyright in a work is infringed by a person who, in New Zealand, other than pursuant to a copyright license:

(a) possesses in the course of a business; or
(b) in the course of a business or otherwise, sells or lets for hire; or
(c) in the course of a business, offers or exposes for sale or hire; or
(d) in the course of a business, exhibits in public or distributes; or
(e) distributes otherwise than in the course of a business to such an extent as to affect prejudicially the copyright owner-an object that is, and that the person knows or has reason to believe is, an infringing copy of the work.

Once again, there is a knowledge requirement for any of these acts, in that the person must know or have reason to believe that the object is an infringing copy of the work. Infringing copy is defined in section 12. 'Business' is defined in section 2 to include a trade or profession.

C. Infringement by Providing Means for Making Infringing Copies

74. Section 37 provides that copyright in a work is infringed by a person who, other than pursuant to a copyright license:[257]

254. Considered in *Burden & Ors v. ESR Group & Ors* [2016] NZHC 1542.
255. Copyright Act 1994 s. 12(5A) in particular.
256. Copyright Act 1994 s. 35.
257. Copyright Act 1994 s. 37(1).

(a) makes; or
(b) imports into New Zealand; or
(c) possesses in the course of a business; or
(d) in the course of a business or otherwise, sells or lets for hire; or
(e) in the course of a business, offers or exposes for sale or hire – an object specifically designed or adapted for making copies of that work, knowing or having reason to believe that the object is to be used to make such infringing copies.

The section also provides that copyright in a work is infringed by a person who, other than under a copyright license, communicates a work to one or more persons, knowing or having reason to believe that infringing copies will be made by means of the reception of the communication in New Zealand or elsewhere.[258]

D. Infringement by Permitting the Use of Premises for an Infringing Performance

75. Section 38 provides that where copyright in a literary, dramatic or musical work is infringed by a performance at a place of public entertainment, any person who gave permission for that place to be used for the performance is also liable for the infringement unless, when the person gave that permission, he or she believed on reasonable grounds that the performance would not infringe copyright. 'Place of public entertainment' includes premises that are occupied mainly for purposes other than public entertainment but are from time to time made available for hire for the purposes of public entertainment.[259]

E. Infringement by Provision of Apparatus for Infringing Performance

76. Section 39 provides that where copyright in a work is infringed by a performance of the work in public, or by the playing or showing of the work in public, by means of apparatus for playing sound recordings; or showing films; or receiving visual images or sounds conveyed by electronic means, then people who supplied the apparatus are liable for infringement if they knew, or had reason to believe, that the apparatus was likely to be so used as to infringe copyright. It also extends to apply to a case of apparatus whose normal use involves a performance, playing, or showing in public, and the person supplying the apparatus had no reasonable grounds for believing that the apparatus would not be so used as to infringe copyright. An occupier of premises who gave permission for the apparatus to be brought onto the premises is also liable for the infringement if, when the occupier gave that permission, he or she knew, or had reason to believe, that the apparatus was likely to be so used as to infringe copyright.[260] The section also provides that a person who supplied a copy of a sound recording or film used to infringe copyright is liable for the infringement if, when the person supplied the copy, he or she knew, or had reason to believe, that the copy

258. Copyright Act 1994 s. 37(2).
259. Copyright Act 1994 s. 38(2).
260. Copyright Act 1994 s. 39(3).

supplied, or a copy made directly or indirectly from the copy, was likely to be used to infringe copyright.

F. Technological Protection Measures

77. The Copyright Act 1994 also contains provisions that protect the use of technological protection measures (TPMs). A TPM means any process, treatment, mechanism, device or system that in the normal course of its operation prevents or inhibits the infringement of copyright in a copyright work that is protected by a TPM.[261] Section 226A provides that a person must not make, import, sell, distribute, let for hire, offer or expose for sale or hire, or advertise for sale or hire, a TPM circumvention device that applies to a technological protection measure if that person knows or has reason to believe that it will, or is likely to, be used to infringe copyright in a TPM work. The provision extends to providing a circumvention service[262] and intentionally publishing information enabling or assisting another person to circumvent a technological protection measure.[263] The issuer of a TPM work has the same rights as a copyright owner has in respect of copyright infringement.[264] The statute also creates an offence of contravening section 226A.[265] There are also related provisions protecting copyright management information.[266]

III. Enforcement and Remedies

78. Traditionally, enforcement of copyright has been a civil matter. However, there has been a growing trend towards the creation of criminal liability for copyright infringement in New Zealand, as has been the case internationally. In addition, there have been recent amendments to the Copyright Act aimed at improving copyright enforcement.[267]

A. Remedies

1. Civil Proceedings

79. The copyright owner and/or the exclusive licensee[268] can bring a civil action for infringement of copyright, and all such relief by way of damages, injunctions, accounts or otherwise is available to the plaintiff as for any other property right.[269]

261. Copyright Act 1994 s. 226.
262. Copyright Act 1994 s. 226A(2).
263. Copyright Act 1994 s. 226A(3).
264. Copyright Act 1994 s. 226B.
265. Copyright Act 1994 s. 226C.
266. Copyright Act 1994 ss 226F–226J.
267. Examples are the Copyright (Infringing File Sharing) Amendment Act 2011 and the Copyright Amendment Act 2011.
268. Copyright Act 1994 s. 123.
269. Copyright Act 1994 s. 120.

There are specific provisions as to damages and order for delivery up to the copyright owner.[270] Application may be made for summary judgment.[271]

Injunctions may be interim or permanent. Interim injunction applications are common in copyright actions. In an application for an interim injunction, a plaintiff must show an arguable case of copyright infringement, and that the balance of convenience favours the plaintiff. The court will then consider the overall justice of the case.[272]

A plaintiff in an action for copyright infringement may be awarded compensatory damages or an account of profits, at the election of the plaintiff. Section 121 contains a provision for innocent infringement. It provides that where it is proved or admitted that at the time of the infringement the defendant did not know, and had no reason to believe, that copyright existed in the work, the plaintiff is not entitled to damages but, without prejudice to the award of any other remedy, is entitled to an account of profits.[273] Damages are generally compensatory.[274] Where infringement is flagrant, a court may award additional damages.[275] Additional damages under section 121(2) cannot be awarded when the plaintiff elects as its principal relief an account of profits.[276] In assessing additional damages, the court is required to have regard to all the circumstances and in particular to the flagrancy of the infringement, and any benefit accruing to the defendant by reason of the infringement.[277] In *Electroquip Ltd & Ors v. Craigco Ltd & Ors*,[278] the Judge said that flagrancy goes beyond mere awareness, and it was not to be found simply because the defendants were unable to prove that they did not know or had no reason to believe that copyright existed in the works.

Remedies are also available for infringement of moral rights, and these include damages and injunctions, and in some circumstances courts can require a disclaimer.[279]

There is an additional provision in relation to unjustified proceedings. Where a person brings proceedings alleging an infringement of copyright, a court may make a declaration that the bringing of proceedings was unjustified and make an order for the payment of damages for any loss suffered by the defendant.[280]

80. From 2011, the Copyright Act also contains a separate enforcement regime for infringing file sharing.[281] The regime enables a copyright rights owner to require

---

270. Copyright Act 1994 ss 121 and 122.
271. Summary judgment was sought in *University of Waikato v. Benchmarking Services Ltd* (2004) 8 NZBLC 101, 561 (CA).
272. *Klissers Farmhouse Bakeries Ltd v. Farmhouse Bakeries Ltd* [1985] 2 NZLR 129.
273. Copyright Act 1994 s. 121(1).
274. *See Electroquip Ltd & Ors v. Craigco Ltd & Ors* (High Court, Auckland, CIV 2006-404-006719, 29 Apr. 2010, Rodney Hansen J), *Oraka Technologies Ltd v. Geostel Vision Ltd* [2016] NZHC 1188.
275. Copyright Act 1994 s. 121(2).
276. *Tiny Intelligence Ltd v. Resport Ltd* [2009] NZSC 35.
277. Copyright Act 1994 s. 121(2).
278. *Electroquip Ltd & Ors v. Craigco Ltd & Ors* (High Court, Auckland, CIV 2006-404-006719, 29 Apr. 2010, Rodney Hansen J).
279. Copyright Act 1994 s. 125.
280. Copyright Act 1994 s. 130.
281. Copyright Act 1994 ss 122A–122U, inserted by the Copyright (Infringing File Sharing) Amendment Act 2011.

an internet service provider (known as Internet Protocol Address Providers in the Act) to issue infringement notices to alleged file sharing infringers. There are three kinds of detection notices, and once an alleged infringer has been given all three notices the rights owner can bring an action in the Copyright Tribunal.[282] Decisions are generally made on the papers.[283] There is a statutory presumption that the information in the infringement notice is correct.[284] The Tribunal can then require the payment of a fine. There is provision in the Act for court suspension of internet accounts, but this provision is not currently in force.[285]

2. Criminal Proceedings

81. The Copyright Act 1994 also contains criminal offences. Making or dealing with infringing objects with knowledge can give rise to criminal liability.[286] Courts can make orders for delivery up in criminal proceedings.[287] Directors and managers of body corporates can also be guilty of a criminal offence if the offence took place with their authority, permission or consent, and they knew or could reasonably be expected to have known that the offence was being committed and failed to take reasonable steps to prevent or stop it.[288]

Other criminal offences in the Copyright Act include offences in relation to technological protection measures and copyright management information.[289] It is also an offence to receive a programme in a communication work with intent to avoid payment.[290]

There are measures in the Copyright Act to strengthen enforcement of copyright offences. These include the Border Protection Measures in Part 7 of the Act, which provide for a regime whereby copyright owners can request that the Customs service detain any pirated copies of works in which they own the copyright. In addition, in 2011 a new part 6A was added to the Copyright Act providing for the appointment of enforcement officers with powers of entry, examination and search. As stated in the Act, an enforcement officer is required, to the extent that is reasonably practicable, to promote compliance with the Act by gathering information relating to and investigating offences under the Act.[291]

282. Copyright Act 1994 s. 122B.
283. Copyright Act 1994 s. 122L.
284. Copyright Act 1994 s. 122N.
285. Copyright Act 1994 s. 122R.
286. Copyright Act 1994 s. 131.
287. Copyright Act 1994 s. 132.
288. Copyright Act 1994 s. 133.
289. Copyright Act 1994 ss 226C and 226J.
290. Copyright Act 1994 s. 227.
291. Copyright Act 1994 s. 134C.

§11. Overlapping and Relation to Other Intellectual Property Laws

82. In New Zealand intellectual property law, there is significant overlap between copyright law and industrial designs law, and there can also be overlap with trade marks law. As explained, copyright law protects artistic works including drawings and models. Industrial designs therefore receive automatic copyright protection. These works may also be eligible for registration under the registered designs law. Copyright works such as logo and packaging designs may also be protected by trade mark law.

Chapter 2. Patents

§1. Sources: Legislation

83. New Zealand patent law has recently had a major overhaul with the passing of the Patents Act 2013. The Patents Act 2013, in force from September 2014, replaces the outdated Patents Act 1953. The new legislation makes some very significant changes to the law, but there is also considerable continuity, and many of the cases decided under the previous legislation will continue to be relevant.

Legislation

The applicable statute is the Patents Act 2013.
Patents granted under the Patents Act 1953 are subject to transitional provisions.[292]
Patents Regulations are expected in 2014.

§2. Patentable Subject Matter

84. Section 13 of the Patents Act 2013 provides that a patent may be granted for an invention only if it is a patentable invention. Section 14 provides that:[293]

> An invention is a 'patentable invention' if the invention, so far as claimed in a claim;
>
> (a) is a manner of manufacture within the meaning of section 6 of the Statute of Monopolies; and
> (b) when compared with the prior art base—
>
> (i) is novel; and
>
> (ii) involves an inventive step; and
>
> (c) is useful; and
> (d) is not excluded from being a patentable invention under section 15 or 16.

To be a patentable subject matter, an invention must therefore satisfy the requirement of being a patentable invention. As defined, this is similar to the requirements under the Patents Act 1953, although the definition is more comprehensive. Significantly, the definition retains the reference to manner of manufacture within the meaning of

292. Patents Act 2013 ss 253–265.
293. Patents Act 2013 s. 14.

section 6 of the Statute of Monopolies, which also means the extensive case law interpreting the meaning of manner of manufacture within the meaning of section 6 of the Statute of Monopolies remains relevant. Section 6 of the Statute of Monopolies (UK) provides as follows:

> VI. Provided also, and be it declared and enacted, that any declaration before mentioned shall not extend to any letters-patent and grants of privilege, for the term of fourteen years or under, hereafter to be made, of the sole working or making of any manner of new manufactures within this realm, to the true and first inventor and inventors of such manufactures, which others at the time of making such letters-patent or grant, shall not use, so as also they be not contrary to the law, nor mischievous to the state, by raising prices of commodities at home, or hurt of trade, or generally inconvenient.

The meaning of manner of manufacture within the meaning of section 6 can only be understood by reference to case law. The New Zealand Court of Appeal considered the meaning of the definition of 'invention', and section 6 of the Statute of Monopolies 1623, in *Wellcome Foundation v. Commissioner of Patents.*[294] Cooke J observed that 'manner of new manufacture' is an expression 'having no ordinary meaning today'. He said that:[295]

> It is a commonplace that the scope of the idea can only be ascertained by seeing how the law has evolved in the decided cases, and that the trend has been to broaden the scope gradually.

New Zealand courts have adopted the approach of the High Court of Australia in *National Research Development Corporation v. Commissioner of Patents*[296] in which the Court took a flexible approach to patentable subject matter. The Court said that any attempt to state the ambit of section 6 by precisely defining 'manufacture' was bound to fail. The purpose of section 6 was to 'allow the use of the prerogative to encourage national development in a field which already, in 1623, was seen to be excitingly unpredictable'. It could never have been sound to attempt to place upon the idea the fetters of an exact verbal formula. The Judges considered the earlier UK decision *Re GEC's Application,*[297] which referred to the need for a vendible product. They concluded that this approach was only made wide enough by understanding the word 'product' as covering every end produced, and treating the word 'vendible' as pointing only to the requirement of utility in practical affairs.

The New Zealand courts are required to interpret the definition of invention with reference to New Zealand's international obligations. New Zealand has international obligations as a signatory to the Paris Convention for the Protection of Industrial

294. [1983] NZLR 385 (CA).
295. *Wellcome Foundation v. Commissioner of Patents* [1983] NZLR 385, 387 (CA).
296. (1959) 102 CLR 252 (HCA). This case was followed in New Zealand in cases including *Wellcome Foundation v. Commissioner of Patents* [1983] NZLR 385 (CA) and *Pharmaceutical Management Agency Ltd v. Commissioner of Patents* [2000] 2 NZLR 529 (CA).
297. (1942) 60 RPC 1.

Property 1883 and the TRIPS Agreement 1994.[298] Article 27(1) of the TRIPS Agreement provides that:[299]

> Subject to the provisions of paragraphs 2 and 3, patents shall be available for any inventions, whether products or processes, in all fields of technology, provided that they are new, involve an inventive step and are capable of industrial application. Subject to paragraph 4 of Article 65, paragraph 8 of Article 70 and paragraph 3 of this Article, patents shall be available and patent rights enjoyable without discrimination as to the place of invention, the field of technology and whether products are imported or locally produced.

In *Pharmaceutical Management Agency Ltd v. Commissioner of Patents*,[300] the Court of Appeal said that under TRIPS Article 27(1), New Zealand had an obligation to make patent protection available 'for any inventions, whether products or processes, in all fields of technology, provided that they are new, involve an inventive step and are capable of industrial application'. The Court in that case extended patentable subject matter to include 'Swiss claims', claims for new uses for known pharmaceutical compounds. However, New Zealand courts continue to exclude methods of medical treatment from the definition of patentable subject matter.[301]

The practice of the Intellectual Property Office of New Zealand (IPONZ) is currently to make patent protection available to a very wide range of subject matter. Items that can be patented include:[302]

- a new product;
- a new process of manufacturing;
- an improvement to an existing product or process;
- a new method or process relating to the testing or control of an existing manufacturing process;
- new chemical compounds or compositions;
- biotechnological matter;
- electrical devices and circuits;
- a second pharmaceutical use for a known chemical compound or composition;
- improvements in computer technology.

85. Exclusions from patentability: The Patents Act 2013 contains a number of express exclusions from patentable subject matter. These include computer software, inventions contrary to public order or morality and other exclusions.

---

298. Agreement on Trade Related Aspects of Intellectual Property Rights 1994.
299. Articles 27(2) and (3) provide for exclusions from patentability.
300. [2000] 2 NZLR 529, 547 (CA).
301. *See* *Pfizer Inc v. Commissioner of Patents* [2005] 1 NZLR 362 (CA).
302. Intellectual Property Office of New Zealand website: *What is a Patent?* http://www.iponz.govt.nz/cms/patents/what-is-a-patent (accessed 9 Apr. 2009).

I. Computer Software

86. Section 11 provides that a computer program is not an invention and not a manner of manufacture for the purposes of this Act,[303] although this applies only to the extent that a claim in a patent or an application relates to a computer program as such.[304] A claim relates to a computer program as such 'if the actual contribution made by the alleged invention lies solely in it being a computer program'.[305]

The effect of this provision is that computer programs 'as such' are excluded from patentability under New Zealand patent law. It does not mean that all computer software is excluded from patentability, and it is likely that a variety of inventions involving computer software will be patentable under section 11. The use of 'as such' makes this provision similar to the provision in Article 52 of the European Patent Convention, meaning that New Zealand law moves closer to the European approach, with the potential for New Zealand courts to draw on European case law.

Section 11(3) will be significant in interpreting whether a computer program is or is not protectable, as it provides that a claim in a patent or an application relates to a computer program as such if the actual contribution made by the alleged invention lies solely in it being a computer program. Section 11(4) goes on to list factors to be taken into account in determining whether the actual contribution made by the alleged invention lies solely in it being a computer program. Section 11(4) provides:

> (4) The Commissioner or the court (as the case may be) must, in identifying the actual contribution made by the alleged invention, consider the following:

(a) the substance of the claim (rather than its form and the contribution alleged by the applicant) and the actual contribution it makes:
(b) what problem or other issue is to be solved or addressed:
(c) how the relevant product or process solves or addresses the problem or other issue:
(d) the advantages or benefits of solving or addressing the problem or other issue in that manner:
(e) any other matters the Commissioner or the court thinks relevant.

Section 11 provides two examples by way of guidance:

> Examples
>
> A process that may be an invention
>
> A claim in an application provides for a better method of washing clothes when using an existing washing machine. That method is implemented through a

303. Patents Act 2013 s. 11(1).
304. Patents Act 2013 s. 11(2).
305. Patents Act 2013 s. 11(3).

computer program on a computer chip that is inserted into the washing machine. The computer program controls the operation of the washing machine. The washing machine is not materially altered in any way to perform the invention.

The Commissioner considers that the actual contribution is a new and improved way of operating a washing machine that gets clothes cleaner and uses less electricity.

While the only thing that is different about the washing machine is the computer program, the actual contribution lies in the way in which the washing machine works (rather than in the computer program per se). The computer program is only the way in which that new method, with its resulting contribution, is implemented.

The actual contribution does not lie solely in it being a computer program. Accordingly, the claim involves an invention that may be patented (namely, the washing machine when using the new method of washing clothes).

A process that is not an invention

An inventor has developed a process for automatically completing the legal documents necessary to register an entity.

The claimed process involves a computer asking questions of a user. The answers are stored in a database and the information is processed using a computer program to produce the required legal documents, which are then sent to the user.

The hardware used is conventional. The only novel aspect is the computer program.

The Commissioner considers that the actual contribution of the claim lies solely in it being a computer program. The mere execution of a method within a computer does not allow the method to be patented. Accordingly, the process is not an invention for the purposes of the Act.

These examples are helpful but represent opposite ends of the spectrum. There will be rather more uncertainty at the margins as to whether any particular computer program is patentable. What is clear is that a variety of computer programs will continue to be patentable under the new legislation. Patent protection will be additional to copyright protection.

II. Inventions Contrary to Public Order or Morality

87. The TRIPS Agreement permits members to exclude from patentability:

> inventions, the prevention within their territory of the commercial exploitation of which is necessary to protect ordre public or morality, including to protect human, animal or plant life or health or to avoid serious prejudice to the environment, provided that such exclusion is not made merely because the exploitation is prohibited by their law.[306]

The New Zealand Patents Act 2013 relies on this provision. Section 15 of the Patents Act 2013 provides that an invention is not a patentable invention if the commercial exploitation of the invention, so far as claimed in a claim, is contrary to public order or morality. The statute gives the following as examples:

- an invention that is a process for cloning human beings;
- an invention that is a process for modifying the germ line genetic identity of human beings;
- an invention that involves the use of human embryos for industrial or commercial purposes;
- an invention that is a process for modifying the genetic identity of animals that is likely to cause them suffering without any substantial medical benefit to human beings or animals, or an invention that is an animal resulting from such a process.

The Patents Act 2013 also establishes a Māori advisory committee.[307] The functions of the Māori advisory committee are to advise the Commissioner on request on whether an invention claimed in a patent application is derived from Māori traditional knowledge or from indigenous plants or animals, and if so, whether the commercial exploitation of that invention is likely to be contrary to Māori values.[308]

In determining whether an invention, is contrary to public order or morality for the purposes of section 15, the Commissioner may, for the purpose of making a decision under this section, seek advice from the Māori advisory committee or any person that the Commissioner considers appropriate.[309]

306. Trade Related Aspects of Intellectual Property Agreement 1994 Art. 27(2).
307. Patents Act 2013 ss 225–228.
308. Patents Act 2013 s. 226.
309. Patents Act 2013 s. 15(3).

III. Other Exclusions

88. Article 27(3) of the TRIPS Agreement also allows members to exclude from patentability:

(a) diagnostic, therapeutic and surgical methods for the treatment of humans or animals;
(b) plants and animals other than micro-organisms, and essentially biological processes for the production of plants or animals other than non-biological and microbiological processes.

Members are required to provide for the protection of plant varieties either by patents or by an effective sui generis system or by a combination.

Section 16 of the Patents Act 2013 provides that:

(1) Human beings, and biological processes for their generation, are not patentable inventions.
(2) An invention of a method of treatment of human beings by surgery or therapy is not a patentable invention.
(3) An invention of a method of diagnosis practised on human beings is not a patentable invention.
(4) A plant variety is not a patentable invention.

The commentary to the Patents Bill as reported from the Parliamentary Select Committee[310] stated that:

> These exclusions would reaffirm that methods of medical treatment are not patentable in New Zealand, support the Royal Commission on Genetic Modification's recommendation to exclude human beings, and incorporate the provisions of Article 27.2 of the World Trade Organisation Agreement on Trade Related Aspects of Intellectual Property Rights.
>
> Article 27.2 requires that it is the commercial exploitation of the invention, rather than the nature of the invention itself, that must be objectionable for this exclusion to be invoked. It is intended that this exclusion would be used infrequently, in relation to inventions where commercial exploitation was likely to be offensive to any significant section of the community, including Māori.

The Patents Act 2013 therefore confirms the earlier common law decisions[311] in excluding methods of medical treatment from patentability. It adds an exclusion for human beings, and biological processes for their generation. 'Swiss claims' for new

310. Patents Bill 235-2, http://www.legislation.govt.nz/bill/government/2008/0235/latest/DLM1419043.html#DLM2843000 (accessed 9 Apr. 2014).

311. *See Wellcome Foundation v. Commissioner of Patents* [1983] NZLR 385 (CA), *Pfizer Inc v. Commissioner of Patents* [2005] 1 NZLR 362 (CA).

uses of known pharmaceutical compounds are however permitted.[312] The Patents Act 2013 also excludes plant varieties, which are protected under the Plant Variety Rights Act 1987.

§3. Conditions of Patentability

89. The new definition of 'patentable invention' in the Patents Act 2013 creates some blurring between the requirements of patentable subject matter and conditions of patentability. Section 13 of the Patents Act 2013 provides that a patent may be granted for an invention only if it is a patentable invention. Section 14 provides that:[313]

> An invention is a 'patentable invention' if the invention, so far as claimed in a claim;

(a) is a manner of manufacture within the meaning of section 6 of the Statute of Monopolies; and
(b) when compared with the prior art base—

- is novel; and
- involves an inventive step; and

(c) is useful; and
(d) is not excluded from being a patentable invention under section 15 or 16.

The requirement that it be a manner of manufacture within the meaning of section 6 of the Statute of Monopolies and the exclusions in sections 15 and 16 have been discussed above under patentable subject matter. The section also includes requirements that an invention be novel and involve an inventive step when compared with the prior art base, and that it be useful.

I. Novelty

90. The Patents Act 1953 set a local novelty standard so that an invention was novel if it was new in New Zealand. The Patents Act 2013 made a major change to the law of novelty, shifting from local novelty to absolute novelty. Section 6 provides that an invention, so far as claimed in a claim, is 'novel' if it does not form part of the prior art base. The prior art base for novelty is defined as 'all matter (whether a product, a process, information about a product or process, or anything else) that has at any time before the priority date of that claim been made available to the public (whether in New Zealand or elsewhere) by written or oral description, by use, or in any other

312. *Pharmaceutical Management Agency Ltd v. Commissioner of Patents* [2000] 2 NZLR 529, 547 (CA).
313. Patents Act 2013 s. 14.

way'.[314] The prior art base for novelty also includes information contained in prior patent specifications that later become public.[315] There are some exceptions, including where disclosure is to be disregarded if it occurred during a one-year period before the filing date and was a consequence of the matter having been obtained unlawfully or in breach of confidence,[316] where disclosure was due to communication to a government department,[317] or due to display at a specified exhibition.[318] There is also an exception for disclosure due to public working for reasonable trial in a one-year period preceding filing, where it is reasonably necessary that the trial be public.[319]

The Patents Act 2013 therefore introduces a new standard of absolute novelty so that any prior art, whether published in New Zealand or elsewhere, will destroy a claim's novelty, meaning that the invention is not a patentable invention. The Act also imposes an obligation on applicants for patents to inform the Commissioner of Patents of the results of any documentary searches by, or on behalf of, a foreign patent office.[320]

II. Inventive Step

91. To be a patentable invention, the invention must involve an inventive step.[321] An invention, so far as claimed in a claim, involves an *inventive step* if it is not obvious to a person skilled in the art, having regard to any matter which forms part of the prior art base.[322] The prior art base for the purpose of assessing whether the invention involves an inventive step is similar but not identical to the prior art base for novelty. For inventive step, the prior art base is defined as:

> all matter (whether a product, a process, information about a product or process, or anything else) that has at any time before the priority date of that claim been made available to the public (whether in New Zealand or elsewhere) by written or oral description, by use, or in any other way.[323]

Unlike that for novelty, the prior art base for inventiveness does not include information contained in prior patent specifications that later become public.[324] The exceptions to disclosure for novelty also apply for inventiveness.[325]

The test for inventive step is established in case law and is not changed by the new statute. It was discussed by the New Zealand Court of Appeal in *Ancare New*

314. Patents Act 2013 s. 8(1).
315. Patents Act 2013 s. 8(2).
316. Patents Act 2013 s. 9(1)(a) and (b).
317. Patents Act 2013 s. 9(1)(c).
318. Patents Act 2013 s. 9(1)(d). 'Specified exhibition' is defined at s. 9(2).
319. Patents Act 2013 s. 9(1)(e).
320. Patents Act 2013 s. 70.
321. Patents Act 2013 s. 14.
322. Patents Act 2013 s. 7.
323. Patents Act 2013 s. 8(1).
324. Patents Act 2013 s. 8(2).
325. Patents Act 2013 s. 9.

Zealand Ltd v. Cyanamid of New Zealand Ltd.[326] Delivering the judgment of the Court of Appeal, Gault J said that the test for obviousness was well established. He said that:

> It postulates a person (or, where appropriate, a team) skilled in the field but not inventive, invested with the common general knowledge available in the field at the priority date, presented with the prior knowledge or prior use relied upon. Prior documents may be looked at together if that is what the skilled person or team would do. It asks whether to that person or team the alleged inventive step would be obvious and would be recognised, without bringing to bear any inventiveness, as something that could be done or is at least worth trying. That is a question of fact. If any embodiment within the scope of the claim is obvious the claim is invalid.

III. Utility

92. Section 14 of the Patents Act 2013 also requires that, in order to be a patentable invention, the invention, so far as claimed in a claim, must be useful. Section 10 provides that an invention, so far as claimed in a claim, is *'useful'* if the invention has a specific, credible and substantial utility. The New Zealand Court of Appeal considered the requirement of utility in *Hammar Maskin AB v. Steelbro New Zealand Ltd.*[327] The Court said that what the invention is intended to do was a matter to be gathered from the specification itself. Where the patentee promises (expressly or impliedly) the attainment of a certain result and this is not obtained, or what is stated as the main object of the invention is not obtained, the patent will be invalid.

§4. Formalities (Procedure for Grant and Obtaining Patent Protection)[328]

93. Any person may apply for a patent, either alone or jointly with another person.[329] Applications must be made in accordance with the Patents Act 2013 and regulations.[330] Patent applications must be accompanied by a complete specification or a provisional specification.[331] If a provisional application is filed, generally a complete

---

326. [2000] 3 NZLR 299 (CA). These principles were approved by the Supreme Court of New Zealand in *Lucas v. Peterson Portable Sawing Systems Ltd* [2006] NZSC 20, [2006] 3 NZLR 721, 733.
327. [2010] NZCA 83.
328. The discussion here is a summary of the process for patent application and grant. There are some additional requirements in relation to Treaty and Convention applications and some additional detailed procedural provisions.
329. Patents Act 2013 s. 31.
330. Patents Act 2013 s. 32.
331. Patents Act 2013 s. 36(1).

specification is required to be filed within one year.[332] The application must be accompanied by a complete specification if the application is a convention application.[333]

Section 39 sets out the requirements for a complete specification. It provides that:[334]

(1) Every complete specification must:

(a) disclose the invention in a manner that is clear enough and complete enough for the invention to be performed by a person skilled in the art; and
(b) disclose the best method of performing the invention that is known to the applicant and for which there is an entitlement to claim protection; and
(c) end with a claim or claims defining the scope of the invention claimed; and
(d) include any other prescribed information.

(2) The claim or claims must:

(a) relate to one invention only; and
(b) be clear and concise; and
(c) be supported by the matter disclosed in the complete specification.

Once a complete specification has been filed, the next step is examination of the application by the IPONZ.[335] The Commissioner of Patents is required to examine the patent application and report whether he or she is satisfied, on the balance of probabilities, that the application and the specification comply with the requirements of this Act and regulations, that the applicant has complied with all requirements, that the invention, so far as claimed, is a patentable invention under section 14, and that there is no other lawful ground of objection to the grant of a patent.[336] If the Commissioner is satisfied that these requirements are met, the Commissioner must accept the specification and publish the acceptance.[337] If the application has not been accepted or abandoned after eighteen months, the Commissioner is required to publish a notice that that complete specification is open to public inspection.[338] In the period after publication and before acceptance, any person may assert that the patent is not a patentable invention on grounds of lack of novelty or inventive step, and must provide reasons.[339] Any person may also request re-examination of the patent in the period between publication and grant.[340]

94. There are provisions for any person to oppose the grant of a patent. The grounds for opposition are set out in section 92. In summary, the grounds are:

332. Patents Act 2013 s. 37.
333. Patents Act 2013 s. 36(1). *See also* s. 53.
334. Patents Act 2013 s. 39.
335. Patents Act 2013 ss 64–70.
336. Patents Act 2013 s. 65.
337. Patents Act 2013 s. 74.
338. Patents Act 2013 s. 76.
339. Patents Act 2013 s. 90.
340. Patents Act 2013 s. 94.

- that the invention is not a patentable invention under section 14;
- that the nominated person is not entitled to the patent;
- that the complete specification does not comply with the specification requirements;
- that the applicant is attempting, or has attempted, to obtain the grant of a patent by fraud, false suggestion or a misrepresentation;
- that the invention was secretly used in New Zealand before the priority date of that claim;
- that granting the patent would be contrary to law.

If grant of a patent is opposed, the Commissioner is required to provide opportunity for a hearing, and consider whether any of the grounds of opposition are established on the balance of probabilities.[341] The Commissioner will then decide whether to grant the patent. If there is no opposition, the patent must be granted after three months has passed since publication of acceptance.[342]

95. The Commissioner may also re-examine a patent application and specification before or after grant, and must do so if requested.[343]

§5. Ownership and Transfer (Assignment-Licenses)

I. Ownership

96. Section 22 of the Patents Act 2013 provides that a patent may only be granted to a person who is the inventor; or derives title from the inventor; or is the personal representative of a deceased person who is the inventor or derived title from the inventor. 'Inventor' means the actual deviser of the invention.[344] A patentee need not be a New Zealand citizen.

A patent may be granted to more than one person, and those people then become co-owners.[345] This will apply in situations such as where a research team makes an invention, and more than one team member is the inventor. Where there are co-owners, each owner is entitled to exercise the exclusive rights given by the patent for the person's own benefit without accounting to the others.[346] However, licenses and assignments can only be made with the agreement of all patentees.[347] There is potential for disputes among owners, and there is power in the statute for the Commissioner to give directions to co-owners.[348]

97. Where an invention is made by an employee, the invention may belong to the employer rather than the employee inventor. Ownership in these circumstances

341. Patents Act 2013 s. 93.
342. Patents Act 2013 s. 101.
343. Patents Act 2013 ss 94–95.
344. Patents Act 2013 s. 5.
345. Patents Act 2013 s. 24.
346. Patents Act 2013 s. 24(2).
347. Patents Act 2013 s. 24(3).
348. Patents Act 2013 ss 26–27.

will depend on the relevant facts and employment contract. The issue was discussed by the New Zealand Court of Appeal in *Empress Abalone Ltd v. Langdon.*[349] Keith J said that there was no dispute between the parties about the law concerning the ownership of inventions in situations such as this. Where an employee made an invention in the course of his employment, which it was part of his duty to make, the law imported into the contract of employment a term that the invention was the property of the employer. The main difficulty was usually that of determining whether the invention concerned was made in the course of the employment, that is, whether it was something that it was the employee's job to invent.

There is potential for dispute between employers and employee inventors. The Patents Act 2013 makes provision for the Commissioner or the Employment Relations Authority to determine disputes of this nature.[350]

II. Transfer

98. A patent is personal property.[351] Patents may be assigned or licensed.[352] A patent may be assigned for the patent area or any place in or part of the patent area.[353] No particular form of license is required by the statute. Licenses and assignments can only be made with the agreement of all patentees.[354]

A person who acquires a patent or share in a patent or an interest in a patent must apply to the Commissioner for registration of that title or interest.[355] Alternatively, the person who disposes of the interest can do this.[356]

§6. Scope of Exclusive Rights

99. The Patents Act 2013 sets out the exclusive rights conferred by grant of a patent. Section 18(1) provides that a patent gives the patentee the exclusive rights, during the term of the patent, to exploit the invention and to authorize another person to exploit the invention. 'Exploit' is defined as including:[357]

(a) if the invention is a product, to:

(1) make, hire, sell or otherwise dispose of the product;
(2) offer to make, hire, sell or otherwise dispose of the product;
(3) use or import the product;

349. [2000] 2 ERNZ 53 (CA).
350. Patents Act 2013 ss 28–30.
351. Patents Act 2013 s. 17.
352. Patents Act 2013 s. 23 and ss 165–168.
353. Patents Act 2013 s. 19.
354. Patents Act 2013 s. 24(3).
355. Patents Act 2013 s. 165(1).
356. Patents Act 2013 s. 165(2).
357. Patents Act 2013 s. 18(2).

(4) keep the product for the purpose of doing any of the things referred to in subparagraphs (i)–(iii); or

(b) if the invention is a process, to use the process or to do any act mentioned in paragraph (a) in respect of a product resulting from that use.

A patent has effect throughout the patent area.[358] The 'patent area' means New Zealand, and New Zealand territorial waters and the airspace above New Zealand and those waters.[359]

The patent term is twenty years from the patent date.[360] The patent date is generally the filing date of the relevant complete specification.[361] However, a patent is not in force until it is granted.[362]

§7. Limitations and Exceptions to the Scope of Patent Protection: Compulsory Licenses

100. The Patents Act 2013 contains substantial provisions in relation to compulsory licenses.[363] There are also provisions for Crown use of inventions.[364]

I. Compulsory Licenses

101. An application for a compulsory license can be made at any time after the later of the expiry of three years from the date that the patent is granted or the expiry of four years from the patent date.[365] Any person may apply to the court for a compulsory license on the grounds that a market for the patent invention is either not being supplied in New Zealand, or is not being supplied on reasonable terms in New Zealand.[366] The court may grant a compulsory license on any terms it sees fit if these grounds are satisfied.[367] If the grounds cease to exist, the license can be terminated by the court.[368]

A compulsory license is not available for a patent for an integrated circuit, or if grant of a license would be contrary to New Zealand's international obligations.[369]

Compulsory licenses granted under the Patents Act provisions are not exclusive and are limited to the supply of the patented invention predominantly in New Zealand.[370]

358. Patents Act 2013 s. 19(1).
359. Patents Act 2013 s. 5.
360. Patents Act 2013 s. 20(1).
361. Patents Act 2013 s. 103(1).
362. Patents Act 2013 s. 103(2).
363. Patents Act 2013 Part 4, Subpart 5.
364. Patents Act 2013 Part 4 Subpart 6.
365. Patents Act 2013 s. 169(1).
366. Patents Act 2013 s. 169.
367. Patents Act 2013 s. 170.
368. Patents Act 2013 s. 170(4).
369. Patents Act 2013 s. 170(2).
370. Patents Act 2013 s. 170(3).

A compulsory license must not be assigned except in connection with the goodwill of the business in which the invention is used.[371]

A person who is granted a compulsory license must pay remuneration to the patentee as agreed between the parties or, where there is no agreement, as determined by the court.[372] A court will only grant a compulsory license if the person applying for the license has made efforts but has been unable to obtain a license on reasonable terms within a reasonable period of time.[373]

There are specific provisions in the Patents Act for compulsory licenses for export of pharmaceutical products in some circumstances.[374]

II. Crown Use of Inventions

102. The Patents Act 2013 provides that any government department, or any person authorized in writing by a government department, may exploit any invention for the services of the Crown at any time after the complete patent specification for the invention has become open to public inspection.[375] Exploitation of the invention will not infringe in these circumstances.[376] Exploitation includes the power to sell any products.[377] The Crown right to use an invention under these provisions is not exclusive.[378] The Crown is replied to pay remuneration.[379]

§8. Duration of Protection: Maintaining and Termination of Patent Protection

103. The term of a patent is twenty years from the patent date, so long as any renewal fees are paid.[380] The patent date is generally the filing date of the complete specification, but there is provision for it to be another date determined under the regulations.[381]

Under the Patents Act 1953 and regulations,[382] patent renewal fees are due in the fourth, seventh, tenth and thirteenth years of the patent, and renewals must be made within six months of the renewal date. It is currently proposed that this renewal structure be changed under the Patents Act 2013, and replaced with an annual renewal fee

371. Patents Act 2013 s. 170(3).
372. Patents Act 2013 s. 175.
373. Patents Act 2013 s. 176.
374. Patents Act 2013 ss 171–175.
375. Patents Act 2013 s. 179.
376. Patents Act 2013 s. 179(2).
377. Patents Act 2013 s. 179(4).
378. Patents Act 2013 s. 186.
379. Patents Act 2013 s. 188.
380. Patents Act 2013 s. 20.
381. Patents Act 2013 s. 103.
382. Patents Regulations 1954, Schedule 1.

chargeable from year four with higher fees in years ten to fourteen and fifteen to twenty.[383]

§9. Infringement and Remedies

I. Infringement

104. Part 4 of the Patents Act 2013 sets out the requirements for patent infringement, with provisions stating what constitutes infringement,[384] and what does not constitute infringement.[385]

It is an infringement of a patent to do anything in the patent area, while the patent is in force, that the patentee has the exclusive right to do, other than with a license, consent or agreement from the patentee.[386] The patentee has the exclusive right to exploit the invention. Where the invention is a product, this includes making, hiring, selling or otherwise disposing of the product, or offering to do any of these things. It also includes using or importing the product, or keeping the product for any of these purposes. If the invention is a process, exploiting the invention includes using the process or to do any of these things in respect of a product resulting from use of the process.[387] There is a presumption that a product is produced by an infringing process where the same product is produced.[388]

It is also an infringement to supply or offer to supply any of the means, relating to an essential element of the invention, for putting the invention into effect. An element of knowledge is required.[389]

105. There are a number of exceptions to infringement. These include the following:

(1) There is an exception for experimental use. It is not an infringement to do an act for experimental purposes relating to the subject matter of an invention.[390] An act for experimental purposes relating to the subject matter of an invention includes an act for the purpose of determining how the invention works, determining the scope of the invention, determining the validity of the claims or seeking an

383. Ministry of Business, Innovation and Employment, *Proposals for Regulations to be made under the Patents Act 2013: Discussion Document* (11 Dec. 2013), at 6, http://www.iponz.govt.nz/cms/pdf-library/patents/patent-regulations-discussion-document-pdf (accessed 9 Apr. 2014).
384. Patents Act 2013 ss 140–142.
385. Patents Act 2013 ss 143–146.
386. Patents Act 2013 s. 140.
387. Patents Act 2013 s. 18.
388. Patents Act 2013 s. 142.
389. Patents Act 2013 s. 141.
390. Patents Act 2013 s. 143.

improvement of the invention (e.g., determining new properties, or new uses, of the invention).[391] This is an exception and new to New Zealand patent law.[392]

(2) There is an exception for prior use. This applies where a person is either exploiting the invention or taking definite steps to exploit it in the patent area immediately before the priority date of the patent.

(3) There is an exception for use of an invention on a foreign vessel, aircraft or vehicle which comes into the patent area temporarily or accidentally.[393]

(4) There is an exception for use to provide information required by law.[394]

The patentee or exclusive licensee may bring a proceeding for infringement.[395] An action can only be brought once the patent is granted.[396]

106. It is common in infringement actions for the defendant to challenge the validity of the patent in a counterclaim for revocation.[397] A counterclaim for revocation of the patent can be made on any of the grounds in section 114. In summary, the grounds are:

- that the invention is not a patentable invention under section 14. This encompasses the requirement that the invention be a manner of manufacture within the meaning of section 6 of the Statute of Monopolies, and the requirements of novelty, inventive step and usefulness;
- that the patentee is not entitled to the patent;
- that the complete specification does not comply with the specification requirements;
- that the patent was obtained by fraud, false suggestion or misrepresentation;
- that the invention, so far as claimed in a claim, was secretly used in New Zealand before the priority date of that claim;
- that the patent has been granted contrary to law.

107. Actions for patent infringement require the plaintiff to establish that the defendant has done an act in the patent area that infringes the exclusive rights of the patentee. In a counterclaim for invalidity on grounds such as lack of novelty or obviousness, a court must determine whether anything encompassed by the relevant claim is not new or obvious.[398]

108. In assessing whether a patent is infringed or invalid, a court will first interpret the patent specification, construing the relevant claims. In construing the claims, the court will take a purposive rather than a purely literal approach.[399] Construction

391. Patents Act 2013 s. 143(2).
392. *See* Ministry of Economic Development, *An Experimental Use Exception for New Zealand's Patent Legislation: An Options Paper*, February 2006, http://www.med.govt.nz/business/intellectual-property/pdf-docs-library/patents/research-exemption-patent-law/options-paper-pdf (accessed 9 Apr. 2014).
393. Patents Act 2013 s. 144.
394. Patents Act 2013 s. 145.
395. Patents Act 2013 s. 148.
396. Patents Act 2013 s. 149.
397. Patents Act 2013 s. 147.
398. *Peterson Portable Sawing Systems Ltd (in liquidation) v. Lucas* [2006] 3 NZLR 721, 729 (SC).
399. *Catnic Components Ltd v. Hill & Smith Ltd* [1981] FSR 60; [1982] RPC 183 (HL).

is a matter of law for the court. The New Zealand Supreme Court said in the case of *Peterson Portable Sawing Systems Ltd (in liquidation) v. Lucas*[400] that:

> A patent specification is to be read as a whole and given a purposive construction. It must be construed as it would be understood by the appropriate addressee – a person skilled in the relevant art. Each part of the specification is to be read objectively in its overall context and in light of the function of that part. The claims were to be interpreted by reference to the object and description in the body of the specification. The claims define the scope of the monopoly conferred by the patent. They limit what others may do. They must clearly define the protected field so others may fairly know where they cannot go. The description in the body of the specification may assist interpretation but it cannot modify the monopoly the inventor has clearly marked out. If his claim is formulated too narrowly so that imitators do not infringe, that cannot be rectified by reference to the description. If it is too wide, consequent invalidity cannot be saved by reading in limitations appearing in the description. The description of a preferred embodiment of the invention is just that and plainly will not confine the scope of an invention claimed more broadly.

The process for assessing infringement involves the court first identifying the essential integers in the claim and then assess whether these integers are present in the alleged infringement. A similar approach is used for invalidity.[401]

II. Remedies

109. The available remedies are injunctions and, at the option of the plaintiff, damages or account of profits.[402] Damages or account of profits must not be awarded in cases of innocent infringement.[403] Innocent infringement occurs where the defendant did not know, and ought not reasonably to have known, that the patent existed. There is a presumption that a person ought reasonably to have known that a patent existed if the product was marked to indicate it was patented in New Zealand and the person knew or ought reasonably to have known of the product.[404] A court may refuse damages or account of profits if patent renewal fees have not been paid.[405] None of the above limitations on damages or account of profits affects the court's power to grant an injunction.[406]

400. [2006] 3 NZLR 721, 729 (SC).
401. Examples of this are in *Assa Abloy New Zealand Limited v. Allegion (New Zealand) Limited* [2016] NZHC 1738, *Doug Andrews Heating & Ventilation Ltd & Anor v. Wayne James Dil & Ors* [2015] NZCA 122.
402. Patents Act 2013 s. 152.
403. Patents Act 2013 s. 153.
404. Patents Act 2013 s. 153(2).
405. Patents Act 2013 s. 155.
406. Patents Act 2013 s. 156.

A person who wishes to exploit an invention may apply to a court for a declaration that exploiting the invention would not infringe.[407]

§10. Overlapping and Relation to Other Intellectual Property Laws

110. There has been some overlap between patentable subject matter and protection offered by other intellectual property regimes. The new exclusions from patentability for computer programs as such, some biotechnological inventions and plant varieties in the Patents Act 2013 will reduce the potential for overlap. Some computer software will however continue to be patentable and also will be protected by copyright under the category of literary works.

407. Patents Act 2013 s. 159.

Chapter 3. Utility Models

111. New Zealand law does not have a regime for utility models.

Chapter 4. Trade Marks

112. In New Zealand law, there is a statutory regime for the protection of registered trade marks. Protection is also available for unregistered trade marks through the tort of passing off and the statutory protection provided by the Fair Trading Act 1986 which prohibits misleading and deceptive conduct in trade. This chapter first outlines the protection for registered trade marks and then the protection for unregistered trade marks.

113. Registered Trade Marks

§1. Sources: Legislation

114. The Trade Marks Act 2002 provides the statutory basis for the protection of registered trade marks. The 2002 Act replaced the Trade Marks Act 1953 which was based on the earlier UK legislation. The 2002 Act also has similarities to the UK legislation, and UK and European case law is therefore relevant to interpretation.

Legislation

The principal statute is the Trade Marks Act 2002.

The main regulations in this field are the Trade Marks Regulations 2003.

In addition to the Trade Marks Act 2002 and regulations, there is a growing body of New Zealand case law interpreting the legislation. Where relevant, New Zealand courts also refer to case law from other jurisdictions, not only particularly from the UK and Europe, but also from jurisdictions such as Australia, Canada and the US.

115. New Zealand is also a party to a number of treaties involving trade marks law. These include the Paris Convention for the Protection of Industrial Property and the Agreement on Trade Related Aspects of Intellectual Property (TRIPS), which requires Member States to have a trade mark registration system and provide minimum levels of protection for trade marks. Amendments were made to the Trade Marks Act in 2011 that enable New Zealand to ratify the Singapore Treaty on the Law of Trademarks (the Singapore Treaty) and to accede to the Protocol Relating to the Madrid Agreement concerning the International Registration of Marks (the Madrid Protocol) and the Nice Agreement Concerning the International Classification of Goods and Services for the Purpose of Registration of Marks (Nice Agreement).

§2. Subject Matter of Protection

I. Signs Which May Serve as Trade Marks

116. The Trade Marks Act 2002 (NZ) provides for a system of protection for registered trade marks in New Zealand. Generally, a trade mark is a distinctive word or symbol which is used in relation to goods or services to show that they are the goods or services of the owner of the trade mark. 'Trade Mark' is defined in the Trade Marks Act 2002, section 5. The definition provides that 'trade mark' means any sign capable of being represented graphically, and capable of distinguishing the goods or services of one person from those of another person. The requirement in the definition of trade mark that the sign be capable of distinguishing the goods or services of one person from those of another person overlaps with the additional requirement of distinctiveness, which is discussed below.

Certification and collective trade marks are included in the definition of trade mark.

The Act also provides a definition of 'sign'.[408] The definition provides that 'sign' includes a brand, colour, device, heading, label, letter, name, numeral, shape, signature, smell, sound, taste, ticket or word; and any combination of signs. The Act does not include definitions of the words listed in the definition. The definition of 'sign' is broad and inclusive. It includes any combination of signs and may include other 'signs' not specifically listed.[409] The definition allows for a wide range of types of marks to be registrable as trade marks, so long as the requirements that they be capable of being represented graphically and capable of distinguishing the goods or services of one person from those of another person are met.

A. Words

117. Word marks are commonly registered, and this can include nouns, adjectives, brand names, or other words so long as these are capable of distinguishing and are not excluded under the absolute or relative grounds for declining registration.[410]

B. Colour

118. Many marks contain elements of colour, for example in device or pictorial marks. Colour marks can also be registered as trade marks in themselves. The *Intellectual Property Office of New Zealand Practice Guidelines* specify that where an applicant seeks to register a colour or colours as a trade mark, they will be required to file either a representation of the colour(s) or a description of the colour(s) using a colour standard. The description should also include information on how the colour or colours are being used or are to be used in relation to goods and services.[411]

---

408. Trade Marks Act 2002 s. 5.
409. Intellectual Property Office of New Zealand, *Introduction to the Trade Marks Act 2002*, February 2012, [6], http://www.iponz.govt.nz/cms/trade-marks/practice-guidelines-index/practice-guidelines/introduction-to-the-trade-marks-act-2002#foot (accessed 9 Apr. 2014).
410. Trade Marks Act 2002 ss 17–30.
411. Intellectual Property Office of New Zealand, *Filing Trade Mark Applications*, 11 Dec. 2012, [4.3.1], http://www.iponz.govt.nz/cms/trade-marks/practice-guidelines-index/practice-guidelines/02-filing-trade-mark-applications (accessed 9 Apr. 2014).

C. *Shapes*

119. Shape marks can include the shape of the goods themselves, or the shape of a container or packaging.[412] Where a three-dimensional shape is registered as a trade mark, the applicant is required to file a representation in a form that clearly shows all of the features of the mark, usually involving multiple aspect views of the shape.[413] A pictorial representation is required rather than a mere description.

D. *Sounds*

120. A sound mark can be any sound, but the sound must be capable of being represented graphically. Musical notation will be accepted as a means of graphical representation.[414] A written description of a sound has also been accepted.[415]

E. *Smells and Tastes*

121. Smell and taste marks are also registrable but must be capable of being represented graphically.

II. Absolute Grounds for Not Registering a Trade Mark

122. In addition to the requirements in the definition of trade mark in the Trade Marks Act 2002, there are a number of absolute and relative grounds for excluding a sign from registration as a trade mark under the Act. Absolute grounds for not registering a trade mark are in sections 17–21, and relative grounds for not registering a trade mark are in sections 22–30. These grounds constitute grounds for the Commissioner of Trade Marks to reject an application for registration.[416] They are also grounds for opposition to an accepted application,[417] and grounds for challenging the validity of a trade mark once registered.[418]

Section 17 provides absolute grounds in general. The main grounds are likelihood of deception or confusion, use contrary to law, likelihood that use or registration would offend a significant section of the community, including Māori, and application made in bad faith. These are discussed below.

---

412. *See* *Fredco Trading Ltd v. Miller* (2006) 11 TCLR 751 (CA) in which the Court of Appeal accepted that the shape of a kiwifruit vine tie could be a trade mark.

413. Intellectual Property Office of New Zealand, *Filing Trade Mark Applications*, 11 Dec. 2012, [4.3.2], http://www.iponz.govt.nz/cms/trade-marks/practice-guidelines-index/practice-guidelines/02-filing-trade-mark-applications (accessed 9 Apr. 2014).

414. Intellectual Property Office of New Zealand, *Filing Trade Mark Applications*, 11 Dec. 2012, [4.3.3], http://www.iponz.govt.nz/cms/trade-marks/practice-guidelines-index/practice-guidelines/02-filing-trade-mark-applications (accessed 9 Apr. 2014).

415. *See* for example Trade Mark No 247094, Unilever Plc (Sunlight detergent 'Squeak') in which the description is 'a squeak produced by the friction of thumb or forefinger on dishware'.

416. Trade Marks Act 2002 s. 43.

417. Trade Marks Act 2002 s. 47.

418. Trade Marks Act 2002 s. 73.

A. *Likelihood of Deception or Confusion*

123. Section 17(1)(a) provides that the Commissioner must not register as a trade mark or part of a trade mark any matter the use of which would be likely to deceive or cause confusion. This requirement is substantially similar to the wording under the Trade Marks Act 1953, so that earlier cases apply. Likelihood of deception or confusion was considered in *Pioneer Hi-Bred Corn Co v. Hy-Line Chicks Pty Ltd.*[419] Richardson J identified several clearly settled propositions, as follows:

(1) The onus is on the applicant for registration of the trade mark to establish that the proposed mark does not offend against section 16, and that onus is discharged on the balance of probabilities.
(2) On an application for registration, the rights of the parties are to be determined as at the date of the application. The evidence as to likelihood of deception or confusion must relate to the position at that time.
(3) The concern is with the possible future use of the mark in respect of goods coming within the specification applied for registration gives the holder protection to that extent.
(4) The section is not concerned with the particular mode of presentation of the product adopted or proposed to be adopted by the applicant, but with the use of the mark in any manner which may be regarded as a fair and proper use of it.
(5) In considering the likelihood of deception or confusion all the surrounding circumstances have to be taken into consideration, including the circumstances in which the applicant's mark may be used, the market in which his goods may be bought and sold and the character of those involved in that market.
(6) But, it is the use of the mark in New Zealand that has to be considered and association of a similar mark with another trader in overseas countries or market is irrelevant, except insofar as it bears on the likelihood of deception or confusion in the New Zealand market.
(7) It is in relation to commercial dealings with goods that the question of deception or confusion has to be considered, and the persons whose states of mind are material are the prospective or potential purchasers of goods of the kind to which the applicant may apply his mark and others involved in the purchase transactions.
(8) For a mark to offend against section 16, it is not necessary to prove that there is a commercial probability of deception leading to a passing off or infringement action. Detriment or financial loss to an opponent need not be established. It is sufficient if the result of the registration of the mark will be that persons to whom the mark is addressed are likely to be deceived or confused. 'Deceived' implies the creation of an incorrect belief or mental impression and causing 'confusion' may go no further than perplexing or mixing up the minds of the purchasing public…Where the deception or confusion alleged is as to the source of the goods, deceived is equivalent to being misled into thinking that the goods bearing the applicant's mark come from some other source and confused to being caused to wonder whether that might not be the case.

419. [1978] 2 NZLR 50 (CA).

(9) The test of likelihood of deception or confusion does not require that all persons in the market are likely to be deceived or confused. But it is not sufficient that someone in the market is likely to be deceived or confused. A balance has to be struck.

(10) Where goods are sold or may be sold to the general public for consumption or domestic use, the Judge or officer making the decision is entitled to take into account his own experience and his own reactions as a member of the public, as well as evidence from other members of the public, when considering whether buyers would be likely to be deceived or confused by use of a trade mark. But where the goods are of a kind not normally sold to the public at large, but are ordinarily sold and expected to be sold in a specialist market consisting of persons engaged in a particular trade, evidence of persons accustomed to dealing in that market as to the likelihood of deception or confusion is essential.

Richardson J held that the object of section 16 was the protection of the relevant New Zealand buying public, not with the protection of the applicant's competitors. He considered that the question was, having regard to the awareness of the opponent's mark in the New Zealand market for goods covered by the registration proposed, would the use of the applicant's mark be likely to deceive or cause confusion to persons in that market.[420]

Likely confusion or deception issues can arise at the examination stage if the trade mark or matter within the trade mark suggests that the goods or services have a specific characteristic or characteristics that the goods or services do not, in fact, have.[421] Likely confusion or deception issues can also arise in cases where there is another trader using the same or a similar mark, and this commonly arises in opposition or invalidity proceedings.

B. Contrary to New Zealand Law

124. Section 17(1)(b) provides that the Commissioner must not register as a trade mark or part of a trade mark any matter the use of which is contrary to New Zealand law or would otherwise be disentitled to protection in any court. This provision can be a ground for rejection at the examination stage or a ground of opposition or a ground in an action for invalidity.

Generally, use of a trade mark will be contrary to New Zealand law where use is in breach of a piece of New Zealand legislation. At the examination stage, examiners consider whether the trade mark consists of or contains matter the use of which is prohibited by a particular piece of legislation, or whether a court decision has issued in respect of the trade mark which establishes the illegality of its use under a particular

420. *Pioneer Hi-Bred Corn Co v. Hy-Line Chicks Pty Ltd* [1978] 2 NZLR 50, 63 (CA). *See also Sexwax Inc v. Zoggs International Ltd* [2014] NZCA 311, [2015] 2 NZLR 1, *Daimler AG v. Sany Group Ltd* [2015] NZCA 418 (2015) 14 TCLR 191, *Cadbury UK Ltd v. J H Whittaker & Sons Ltd* [2014] NZHC 816.

421. *See* Intellectual Property Office of New Zealand, *Absolute Grounds: General*, [2], http://www.iponz.govt.nz/cms/trade-marks/practice-guidelines-index/practice-guidelines/04-absolute-grounds-general-2/2-deception-or-confusion (accessed 9 Apr. 2014).

piece of legislation. Examples of particular pieces of legislation that prohibit the use of particular marks are the Geneva Conventions Act 1958 and the Flags, Emblems, and Names Protection 1981. The Fair Trading Act 1986 is an example of legislation under which a court decision may have issued establishing the illegality of use of a mark.[422]

Section 17(1)(b) also provides that the Commissioner must not register as a trade mark or part of a trade mark any matter, the use of which would otherwise be disentitled to protection in any court. The IPONZ Guidelines state that this primarily applies to trade marks whose use would give rise to the common law action of passing off, or whose use would amount to a breach of copyright, and that these matters are more properly determined in a court. In light of this, only in exceptional circumstances will IPONZ reject an application on the grounds that the use of the mark 'would otherwise be disentitled to protection in any court'.

C. Use or Registration Likely to Offend a Significant Section of the Community, Including Māori

125. Section 17(1)(c) provides that the Commissioner must not register as a trade mark or part of a trade mark any matter the use or registration of which would, in the opinion of the Commissioner, be likely to offend a significant section of the community, including Māori.

This section, as now worded, was new in the 2002 Act and has not yet come before the New Zealand courts. It is a ground for objection at the examination stage, ground for opposition, and ground for a challenge to validity under section 73.

The first issue is the meaning of 'likely to offend a significant section of the community'. The IPONZ *Guidelines* refer to a number of cases from the United Kingdom for guidance,[423] and conclude that a distinction should be drawn between marks that are offensive and marks that would be considered by some to be in poor taste. The *Guidelines* provide that:[424]

> When considering whether the use or registration of a trade mark 'would be likely to offend a significant section of the community', examiners should note that:

- Each case must be decided on its own merits.
  - The question must be considered as at the date of application.

422. *See* Intellectual Property Office of New Zealand, *Absolute Grounds: General*, [3], http://www.iponz.govt.nz/cms/trade-marks/practice-guidelines-index/practice-guidelines/04-absolute-grounds-general-2/3-contrary-to-law (accessed 9 Apr. 2014).
423. These include HALLELUJAH Trade Mark [1976] RPC 605, Ghazilian's Trade Mark Application [2002] RPC 628 and Dick & Fanny, Case R 111/2002-4.
424. Intellectual Property Office of New Zealand, *Absolute Grounds: General*, [4.1], http://www.iponz.govt.nz/cms/trade-marks/practice-guidelines-index/practice-guidelines/04-absolute-grounds-general-2/4-offensive-trade-marks/4-1-likely-to-offend-a-significant-section-of-the-community (accessed 9 Apr. 2014).

- The question must be considered objectively, from the point of view of 'right-thinking members of the public'.
- The application should not be rejected merely because the mark is considered to be in poor taste.
- A mark should be considered 'likely to offend a significant section of the community' where:
- The mark is likely to cause a significant section of the community to be outraged; and/or
- A significant section of the community is likely to feel that the use or registration of the mark should be the subject of censure.
- A significant section of the community is likely to feel that the mark should be the subject of censure where the mark is likely to undermine current religious, family or social values.
- The significant section of the community may be a minority that is nevertheless substantial in number.
- A higher degree of outrage or censure among a smaller section of the community, or a lesser degree of outrage or censure among a larger section of the community, may suffice.

The second issue is the meaning of 'likely to offend a significant section of the community, including Māori'. Section 17(1)(c) makes specific reference to Māori as a specific section of the community to whom the provision can apply. It was passed in response to long-standing objections by Māori about registration and use of trade marks containing Māori imagery. The section provides an avenue to prevent registration of these kinds of offensive marks.

126. Sections 177–180 require that the Commissioner appoint an advisory committee to advise the Commissioner whether the proposed use or registration of a trade mark that is, or appears to be, derivative of a Māori sign, including text and imagery, is, or is likely to be, offensive to Māori. Members of the advisory committee are required to knowledge of te ao Māori (Māori worldview) and tikanga Māori (Māori protocol and culture).[425]

Section 170 provides a broad appeal right from any decision of the Commission, providing that a person who is aggrieved by a decision of the Commissioner under the Act may appeal to the court. Section 73 provides that an 'aggrieved person (which includes a person who is culturally aggrieved)' may apply for a declaration that the registration of a trade mark is invalid, and the Commissioner or the court may make such a declaration. These also provide avenues for appeal against registration of offensive marks.

D. Bad Faith

127. Section 17(2) provides that the Commissioner must not register a trade mark if the application is made in bad faith. There is no statutory definition of bad faith, but it has a potentially broad application. It covers disputed ownership of the mark, dishonesty or fraud, and issues of intention to use the mark.

425. Trade Marks Act 2002 s. 179(2).

The IPONZ *Guidelines* advise that examiners may raise concerns under this section if it seems very likely that the applicant is not the owner of the trade mark that is the subject of the application, but advise that this situation would usually only arise where the trade mark was well known as being the trade mark of a particular company or individual, and there was no apparent relationship between the applicant and the known owner of the trade mark.[426]

Bad faith can also be a ground for opposition and validity challenges under section 73, and it is likely that issues such as dishonesty or absence of intention to use the mark would arise in this context.[427]

E. Section 18: Distinctiveness

128. Section 18 of the Trade Marks Act 2002 provides:

(1) The Commissioner must not register:

(a) a sign that is not a trade mark:
(b) a trade mark that has no distinctive character:
(c) a trade mark that consists only of signs or indications that may serve, in trade, to designate the kind, quality, quantity, intended purpose, value, geographical origin, time of production of goods or of rendering of services, or other characteristics of goods or services:
(d) a trade mark that consists only of signs or indications that have become customary in the current language or in the bona fide and established practices of trade.

(2) The Commissioner must not refuse to register a trade mark under subsection (1)(b), (c), or (d) if, before the date of application for registration, as a result of either the use made of it or of any other circumstances, the trade mark has acquired a distinctive character.

Section 18 covers a number of potentially overlapping requirements which together cover the requirement of distinctiveness. Section 18 requirements can function as grounds for rejection of registration at the examination stage, ground for opposition and ground for a validity challenge under section 73.

1. Sign That Is Not a Trade Mark

129. Section 18(1)(a) provides that the Commissioner must not register a sign that is not a trade mark. As discussed, the definition of 'trade mark' in section 5 requires that it be a 'sign' as defined. The definition of 'sign' includes a brand, colour, device, heading, label, letter, name, numeral, shape, signature, smell, sound, taste, ticket or

426. Intellectual Property Office of New Zealand, *Absolute Grounds: General*, [5], http://www.iponz.govt.nz/cms/trade-marks/practice-guidelines-index/practice-guidelines/04-absolute-grounds-general-2/5-bad-faith (accessed 9 Apr. 2014).
427. *See* discussion in Paul Sumpter, *Trade Marks in Practice* 50–59 (3rd ed., CCH N.Z. Ltd. 2015).

word; and any combination of signs.[428] To be a trade mark, a sign must also be capable of being represented graphically, and capable of distinguishing the goods or services of one person from those of another person.

A trade mark application can therefore fail under section 18(1)(a) on the grounds that it is not a sign, is not capable of being represented graphically, or is not capable of distinguishing. However the requirement that the sign be capable of distinguishing does present some interpretation issues, as it appears to overlap with the requirement of distinctiveness in section 18(1)(b), and this issue has not yet been clarified by case law. The IPONZ *Guidelines* state that rejections under section 18(1)(a) on the grounds that that the sign is incapable of distinguishing the applicant's goods or services from those of other traders will be uncommon.[429]

2. No Distinctive Character

130. Section 18(1)(b) provides that the Commissioner must not register a trade mark that has no distinctive character. As noted, this overlaps with section 18(1)(a). It also overlaps with the more specific provisions in section 18(1)(c) and (d).

The distinctiveness provisions in the 2002 Act were considered by the New Zealand Court of Appeal in *Intellectual Reserve Inc v. Robert Sintes.*[430] In that case, Baragwanath J noted that Jacob J in *British Sugar PLC v. James Robertson & Sons Ltd*[431] said that there was no material difference in effect between the adverb 'distinguishing' in section 5 and the adjective 'distinctive' in section 18(1)(b). Baragwanath J said that the section 5 requirement that the mark be capable of distinguishing meant that the mark must at the date of registration have that as an inherent quality or have it demonstrated in fact by prior use or other circumstances. He said that the requirement in section 18(1)(b) meant that a sign which was capable of distinguishing the goods and services as having a particular trade origin (section 5) must actually do so; it must at the time of the application be of such character as effects such distinction. Baragwanath J said that 'distinctive' was not defined in the 2002 Act, but that the best test of what form of distinctiveness was required remained that formulated by Lord Parker in *The Registrar of Trade Marks v. W&G du Cros Ltd*[432] [1913] AC 624 Lord Parker said:

> In my opinion, in order to determine whether a mark is distinctive it must be considered quite apart from the effects of registration. The question, therefore, is whether the mark itself, if used as a trade mark, is likely to become actually distinctive of the goods of the person so using it. The applicant for registration in effect says, 'I intend to use this mark as a trade mark, i.e., for the purpose of

428. Trade Marks Act 2002 s. 5.
429. Intellectual Property Office of New Zealand, s. 18 of the Trade Marks Act 2002 *Absolute Grounds: Distinctiveness*, [2.2], http://www.iponz.govt.nz/cms/trade-marks/practice-guidelines-index/practice-guidelines/05-absolute-grounds-distinctiveness-section-18-of-the-trade-marks-act-2002#bookmark2. (accessed 9 Apr. 2014).
430. [2009] NZCA 305, (Arnold, Ellen France and Baragwanath JJ).
431. 1996 R.P.C. 281 (Ch).
432. [1913] AC 624.

> distinguishing my goods from the goods of other persons,' and the Registrar or the Court has to determine before the mark be admitted to registration whether it is of such a kind that the applicant, quite apart from the effects of registration, is likely or unlikely to attain the object he has in view. The applicant's chance of success in this respect must, I think, largely depend upon whether other traders are likely, in the ordinary course of their business and without any improper motive, to desire to use the same mark, or some mark nearly resembling it, upon or in connection with their own goods. It is apparent from the history of trade marks in this country that both the Legislature and the Courts have always shown a natural disinclination to allow any person to obtain by registration under the Trade Marks Acts a monopoly in what others may legitimately desire to use. For example, names (unless represented in some special manner) and descriptive words have never been recognized as appropriate for use as trade marks.

Baragwanath J said that the statutory test is to be applied at the time of the application for registration, and that the application may be before the goods or services have been put on the market. Distinctiveness cannot be confined to the factual position at that point; the crucial question was the inherent potential of the mark to serve as a distinguishing feature. The Judge concluded that, for a sign to be distinctive:[433]

(a) it must not be commonplace, but must be distinctive of the user;
(b) it must not infringe the statute;
(c) it must not be such as other traders are likely to wish to use for competing goods or services;
(d) the use of a disclaimer may bear on the acceptability of a mark;
(e) there should be a realistic construction of the mark and its specification in the relevant market.

Baragwanath J said that the judgment cannot be influenced by what its author means by the sign or what a layman says concerning its legal effect. The test was one of the perceptions of the average consumer having regard to the various methods and practice of advertising they are likely to encounter. Such a consumer was likely to perceive a mark as a whole rather than analyse its various details.

The IPONZ *Guidelines* provide guidelines to examiners on assessing distinctiveness.[434] They quote from *'Cycling IS ...' Trade Mark Applications*, as follows:[435]

- The question whether a particular sign possesses a distinctive character cannot be considered in the abstract. It must be considered in relation to the goods or services for which registration is sought.

433. *Intellectual Reserve Inc v. Robert Sintes* [2009] NZCA 305, [35].
434. Intellectual Property Office of New Zealand, s. 18 of the Trade Marks Act 2002 *Absolute Grounds: Distinctiveness*, [3.23], http://www.iponz.govt.nz/cms/trade-marks/practice-guidelines-index/practice-guidelines/05-absolute-grounds-distinctiveness-section-18-of-the-trade-marks-act-2002#bookmark2 (accessed 9 Apr. 2014).
435. [2002] RPC 729, 743–744.

- The mark must possess enough of a distinctive character to be regarded as an indication of trade origin by the relevant class of persons or at least a significant proportion thereof.
- The relevant class of persons consists of the trade and average consumers of the specified goods and services in the territory covered by the application for registration.
- The average consumer of the goods or services concerned is to be regarded as reasonably well-informed and reasonably observant and circumspect.
- It is to be remembered that the average consumer normally perceives a mark as a whole and does not proceed to analyse its various details.
- The average consumer's level of attention is likely to vary according to the category of goods or services in question.
- The perceptions of the average consumer must be assessed in context, with due regard for the realities of the market place. It will be relevant to have regard to the various methods and practices of marketing that the average consumer of the relevant goods or services is likely to encounter under normal and fair trading conditions.

3. Section 18(1)(c)

131. Section 18(1)(c) provides that the Commissioner must not register a trade mark that consists only of signs or indications that may serve, in trade, to designate the kind, quality, quantity, intended purpose, value, geographical origin, time of production of goods or of rendering of services, or other characteristics of goods or services.

This section prevents marks that are descriptive of goods or services or some characteristic of those goods or services, and includes marks that are generic.[436] The IPONZ *Guidelines* state that for the provision to apply, there must be a reasonable likelihood that the mark will be associated, in the mind of the relevant class of persons, with a characteristic or characteristics of the goods or services.[437] The test is stated as being 'would the average consumer regard the mark as a normal way of designating a characteristic or characteristics of the goods or services in question?'[438]

---

436. Intellectual Property Office of New Zealand, s. 18 of the Trade Marks Act 2002, *Absolute Grounds: Distinctiveness*, [4.1], http://www.iponz.govt.nz/cms/trade-marks/practice-guidelines-index/practice-guidelines/05-absolute-grounds-distinctiveness-section-18-of-the-trade-marks-act-2002#bookmark2 (accessed 9 Apr. 2014).
437. Intellectual Property Office of New Zealand, s. 18 of the Trade Marks Act 2002, *Absolute Grounds: Distinctiveness*, [4.2.2], http://www.iponz.govt.nz/cms/trade-marks/practice-guidelines-index/practice-guidelines/05-absolute-grounds-distinctiveness-section-18-of-the-trade-marks-act-2002#bookmark2 (accessed 9 Apr. 2014).
438. Intellectual Property Office of New Zealand, s. 18 of the Trade Marks Act 2002 *Absolute Grounds: Distinctiveness*, [4.2.5], http://www.iponz.govt.nz/cms/trade-marks/practice-guidelines-index/practice-guidelines/05-absolute-grounds-distinctiveness-section-18-of-the-trade-marks-act-2002#bookmark2 (accessed 9 Apr. 2014).

4. Section 18(1)(d)

132. Section 18(1)(d) provides that the Commissioner must not register a trade mark that consists only of signs or indications that have become customary in the current language or in the bona fide and established practices of trade.

This provision prevents registration of signs that other traders customarily use. It overlaps significantly with the other distinctiveness provisions.[439]

5. Section 18(2): Acquired Distinctiveness

133. Section 18(2) provides that the Commissioner must not refuse to register a trade mark under subsection 18(1)(b), (c), or (d) if, before the date of application for registration, as a result of either the use made of it or of any other circumstances, the trade mark has acquired a distinctive character. This allows for a mark that is not inherently distinctive to acquire distinctiveness through use. The onus is on the applicant for registration to provide evidence of acquired distinctiveness.[440]

Acquired distinctiveness through use under section 18(2) in relation to a kiwifruit vine tie was found in *Fredco Trading Ltd v. Miller.*[441] The Court of Appeal reviewed the evidence and concluded that it was sufficient to show that the mark was being used as a 'badge of origin'.[442]

III. Relative Grounds for Not Registering a Trade Mark

134. In addition to absolute grounds for not registering a trade mark, sections 22–30 provide for a number of relative grounds for not registering, generally involving conflict with other marks.

One significant provision in this group is section 25. Section 25[443] generally provides that the Commissioner must not register a trade mark in respect of any goods or services if:

(a) it is identical to a trade mark belonging to a different owner and that is registered, or has priority in respect of the same goods or services; or in respect of goods or services that are similar to those goods and services, and its use is likely to deceive or confuse; or
(b) it is similar to a trade mark that belongs to a different owner and that is registered, or has priority, in respect of the same goods or services or goods or services that

439. These issues were raised in *AA Insurance Ltd & Ors v. AMI Insurance Ltd* [2012] 1 NZLR 837 (HC).

440. Intellectual Property Office of New Zealand, *Overcoming Section 18,* http://www.iponz.govt.nz/cms/trade-marks/practice-guidelines-index/practice-guidelines/05a-overcoming-section-18#22 (accessed 9 Apr. 2014).

441. (2006) 11 TCLR 751 (CA).

442. *See also Advantage Group Ltd & Ors v. Advantage Computers Ltd* [2002] 3 NZLR 741 (CA).

443. Section 25 is subject to s. 26 exceptions which include consent and honest concurrent use.

are similar to those goods or services, and its use is likely to deceive or confuse; or

(c) it is, or an essential element of it is, identical or similar to, or a translation of, a trade mark that is well-known in New Zealand whether through advertising or otherwise, in respect of those goods or services or similar goods or services or any other goods or services if the use of the trade mark would be taken as indicating a connection in the course of trade between those other goods or services and the owner of the well-known trade mark, and would be likely to prejudice the interests of the owner.

Application of section 25 requires assessment of whether trade marks are identical or similar, whether goods or services are identical or similar and of likelihood of deception or confusion. In relation to similarity of marks, the New Zealand courts have generally applied variants of the test in *Re Pianotist Co's Application*,[444] where Parker J said:

> You must take the two words. You must judge of them, both by their look and by their sound. You must consider the nature and kind of customer who would be likely to buy those goods. In fact, you must consider all the surrounding circumstances; and you must further consider what is likely to happen if each of those trade marks is used in a normal way as a trade mark for the goods of the respective owners of the marks.

The IPONZ *Guidelines* also use the *Re Pianotist* test, which has evolved into the following guidelines:[445]

- The marks should be compared as a whole.
- Imperfect recall must be taken into account.
- The idea of the mark is important.
- The look and sound of the mark must be considered.
- The trade channels of the respective goods and/or services must be taken into account.

In relation to similarity of goods and services, courts use the approach taken in *British Sugar PLC v. James Robertson & Sons Ltd.*[446] In that case, the Judge was required to consider whether the two marks were used for similar goods. The Judge noted that the wider the scope of the concept, the wider the absolute scope of protection of a mark. He said that, in effect, a registration covers the goods of the specification plus similar

444. (1906) 23 RPC 774 at 777. The test was used in *Austin, Nichols & Co. Inc v. Stichting Lodestar* [2007] NZSC 103, [2008] 2 NZLR 141 (SC). *See also NV Sumatra Tobacco Trading Co v. New Zealand Milk Brands Ltd* [2011] NZCA 264; [2011] 3 NZLR 206.

445. Intellectual Property Office of New Zealand, *Practice Guidelines: Relative grounds: Identical or similar marks,* [4], http://www.iponz.govt.nz/cms/trade-marks/practice-guidelines-index/practice-guidelines/10-relative-grounds-identical-or-similar-trade-marks/4-similar-trade-marks (accessed 9 Apr. 2014).

446. 1996 R.P.C. 281 (Ch), applied in *NV Sumatra Tobacco Trading Co v. New Zealand Milk Brands Ltd* [2011] NZCA 264; [2011] 3 NZLR 206.

goods. No one may use the registered mark or a similar mark for any of those goods unless he has some other defence. This suggested a need for caution, as otherwise, however narrow a specification, the actual protection will be wide. The Judge said that the following factors must be relevant in considering whether there is or is not similarity of goods:

(1) The respective uses of the respective goods or services.
(2) The respective users of the respective goods or services.
(3) The physical nature of the goods or acts of service.
(4) The respective trade channels through which the goods or services reach the market.
(5) In the case of self-serve consumer items, where in practice they are respectively found or likely to be found in supermarkets and in particular whether they are, or are likely to be, found on the same or different shelves.
(6) The extent to which the respective goods or services are competitive. This inquiry may take into account how those in trade classify goods, for instance whether market research companies, who of course act for industry, put the goods or services in the same or different sectors.

The IPONZ *Guidelines* also use the *British Sugar* approach, and suggest the following questions which may be helpful when considering whether goods or services are 'similar' to other goods or services:[447]

- How will the goods or services be used? What is their purpose? If the goods or services are not identical but could be used together, or at the same time, or in the same way, or to achieve the same purpose, the public may see them as related and therefore assume that they originate from the same entity.
- How likely is it that the same entity would produce or provide the goods or services?
- Would the goods or services usually be provided or sold in the same types of outlets?
- In the case of self-serve consumer items, would the goods usually be found in the same place in the retail outlet, or on the same shelves?
- Would the goods and/or services usually be provided to the same class or classes of customer?
- How similar are the lines of business of the respective traders?
- How broad are the respective specifications of goods/services? If a trader offers a very narrow, specialized range of goods or services, there is less likelihood that consumers would expect that trader to produce or provide different goods or services. Alternatively, if a trader offers a very wide range of goods or services, consumers may associate almost any goods or services with that trader.

---

447. Intellectual Property Office of New Zealand, *Practice Guidelines: Relative grounds: Identical or similar marks,* [6], http://www.iponz.govt.nz/cms/trade-marks/practice-guidelines-index/practice-guidelines/10-relative-grounds-identical-or-similar-trade-marks/6-similarity-of-the-goods-or-services (accessed 9 Apr. 2014).

- How expensive are the goods or services? Consumers are likely to pay more attention when selecting expensive items than when selecting inexpensive ones. There may therefore be less likelihood of deception or confusion in relation to expensive goods or services.
- Are the goods or services in competition with each other?

In assessing likelihood of deception or confusion, IPONZ applies the following test:[448]

> Assuming use by [the owner of the cited mark] of its trade mark [X] in a normal and fair manner for [the goods or services in the specification of the cited mark], is the [Court or Commissioner] satisfied that there would be a reasonable likelihood of deception or confusion among a substantial number of persons if the applicant's trade mark [Y] was used in a normal and fair manner for [the goods or services in the specification of the application under consideration]?

This is also broadly the approach of the New Zealand courts, and the above test was applied in the recent New Zealand Court of Appeal decision *Intellectual Reserve Inc v. Robert Sintes*.[449]

Section 25(1)(c) provides that the Commissioner must not register a trade mark in respect of any goods or services if it is identical or similar to a trade mark that is well known in New Zealand, if it would be taken as indicating a connection in the course of trade with the well-known mark and would be likely to prejudice the interests of the owner. This means that a mark can be denied registration even where there is no confusion if the mark is similar to a well-known mark. It extends the protection for well-known marks.[450]

IV. Different Categories of Marks

135. The definition of 'trade mark' in the Trade Marks Act 2002 includes a certification trade mark and a collective trade mark.

Under section 5 of the Trade Marks Act 2002, a 'certification trade mark' means a sign capable of:

(a) being represented graphically; and
(b) distinguishing, in the course of trade:

448. From *Hannaford & Burton Ltd v. Polaroid Corporation* [1976] 2 NZLR 14 at 18. The approach to confusion and deception taken by Richardson J in *Pioneer Hi-Bred Corn Co v. Hy-Line Chicks Pty Ltd* [1978] 2 NZLR 50 (CA) is also relevant here.

449. [2009] NZCA 305, (Arnold, Ellen France and Baragwanath JJ). *See also Daimler AG v. Sany Group Ltd* [2015] NZCA 418 (2015) 14 TCLR 191.

450. *NV Sumatra Tobacco Trading Co v. New Zealand Milk Brands Ltd* [2011] NZCA 264; [2011] 3 NZLR 206. *See also Daimler AG v. Sany Group Ltd* [2015] NZCA 418 (2015) 14 TCLR 191, *Tomtom Comunications Ltd v. Tomtom International B V* [2015] NZHC 3333 (2015) 14 TCLR 272.

(1) goods certified by any person in respect of origin, material, mode of manufacture, quality, accuracy, or other characteristic from goods not so certified; or
(2) services certified by any person in respect of quality, accuracy, performance, or other characteristic from services not so certified.

A certification trade mark is not a badge of origin but identifies that goods or services have been certified in relation to particular characteristics. A certification trade mark may be registered in the name of the person certifying the goods or services but may not be registered in the name of a person who carries on a trade in goods or services of the kind certified.[451]

Under section 5 of the Trade Marks Act 2002, a 'collective trade mark' means a sign capable of:

(a) being represented graphically; and
(b) distinguishing the goods or services of members of the collective association that is the owner of the sign from those of persons who are not members of the collective association.

A collective association means a body (whether incorporated or not) that has or is able to have members, and is constituted for the joint benefit of its members and its membership at any time can be ascertained.[452]

§3. Conditions of Protection

136. A trade mark may be registered in respect of particular goods and/or services within one or more classes.[453] Before registering a trade mark, the Commissioner of Trade Marks undertakes an examination and must be satisfied that there are no absolute or relative grounds that would prevent registration.[454] If all of the requirements for registration are met, the Commissioner must, subject to any conditions the Commissioner thinks fit, accept the application.[455] There is then an opportunity for opposition, which, if successfully resolved in favour of the applicant, is followed by registration.[456]

Registration lasts for ten years, after which renewal is required.[457] Registration can be cancelled if not renewed. It can also be cancelled or altered for failure to comply with a condition.[458] Conditions include the requirement of a disclaimer.[459]

137. Registration can be revoked on any of the following grounds:[460]

451. Trade Marks Act 2002 s. 14.
452. Trade Marks Act 2002 s. 5.
453. Trade Marks Act 2002 s. 13(1).
454. Trade Marks Act 2002 s. 13.
455. Trade Marks Act 2002 s. 40.
456. Trade Marks Act 2002 s. 50.
457. Trade Marks Act 2002 ss 57–58.
458. Trade Marks Act 2002 s. 62.
459. Trade Marks Act 2002 s. 71.
460. Trade Marks Act 2002 s. 66.

- a continuous period of three years or more of non-use, in relation to goods or services in respect of which it is registered, unless the non-use is due to special circumstances that are outside the control of the owner;
- that the mark has become generic;
- that the article or substance was formerly manufactured under a patent or the service was formerly a patented process; and two years or more has elapsed since the expiry of the patent; and the word is or the words are the only practicable name or description of the article, substance, or service;
- that, as a result of use by the owner or with the owner's consent in relation to the goods or services in respect of which the trade mark is registered, the trade mark is likely to deceive or confuse the public, for instance as to the nature, quality, or geographical origin of those goods or services.

An aggrieved person may apply to the Commissioner or the court for the revocation of registration, but vexatious applications may be refused.[461]

§4. Formalities (Procedure for Obtaining Protection, Establishing and Maintaining Trade Marks)

138. While it is not essential to register a trade mark under the Trade Marks Act 2002, registered trade marks are accorded greater protection than unregistered trade marks. Unregistered trade marks are protected by the common law.

The process for obtaining a registered trade mark is set out in Part 3 of the Trade Marks Act 2002 and in the Trade Mark Regulations 2003. Application for registration can be made in respect of particular goods or/and services within one or more classes.[462] The Commissioner must not register a trade mark in respect of all of the goods or services included in a class, or a large variety of goods or services, unless the specification is justified by the use or intended use of the sign.[463]

Before registering a trade mark, the Commissioner of Trade Marks undertakes an examination[464] and must be satisfied that there are no absolute or relative grounds that would prevent registration.[465] If all of the requirements for registration are met, the Commissioner must, subject to any conditions the Commissioner thinks fit, accept the application.[466] If the application does not comply, the Commissioner must inform the applicant and give the applicant an opportunity to respond or amend the application.[467] The Commissioner must reject an application if, within the time specified by the Commissioner, the applicant does not satisfy the Commissioner that the applicant has complied with the requirements for registering a trade mark.[468]

461. Trade Marks Act 2002 s. 65.
462. Trade Marks Act 2002 s. 32.
463. Trade Marks Act 2002 s. 32(2).
464. Trade Marks Act 2002 s. 39.
465. Trade Marks Act 2002 s. 13.
466. Trade Marks Act 2002 s. 40.
467. Trade Marks Act 2002 s. 41.
468. Trade Marks Act 2002 s. 43.

Once an application is accepted, it is advertised,[469] and there is then an opportunity for opposition.[470] The applicant is required to provide a counter-statement.[471] The Commissioner then holds a hearing if required and determines whether and subject to what conditions the trade mark is to be registered.[472] If opposition proceedings are successfully resolved in favour of the applicant, the trade mark is then registered.[473]

§5. Ownership and Transfer (Assignment, Licenses)

I. Ownership and Transfer

139. A registered trade mark is a personal property,[474] as is an application for registration of a trade mark.[475] A trade mark is assignable and transmittable in respect of all or some of the goods or services for which it is registered.[476] Section 10(1) provides that the owner of a registered trade mark has the exclusive right to assign or transmit the registered trade mark, either in connection with the goodwill of a business or not. 'Owner' is defined in section 5(1) in relation to a registered trade mark as the person in whose name the trade mark is registered.[477]

If title to a trade mark is assigned or transmitted after the date the trade mark is registered, either the registered owner or the person to whom the trade mark is assigned or transmitted may apply to the Commissioner to register the new owner's title.[478] The Commissioner is then required to register the new owner.[479]

II. Licensing

140. Under earlier legislation, there was an extensive system for registration of licenses, and this no longer exists. However, the 2002 Act does contain provisions relating to licensing. Section 10(1) provides that the owner of a registered trade mark has the exclusive right to authorize other persons to use the registered trade mark. 'Licensee' is defined in the Act in relation to a trade mark to mean a person whose use

469. Trade Marks Act 2002 s. 46.
470. Trade Marks Act 2002 s. 47.
471. Trade Marks Act 2002 s. 48.
472. Trade Marks Act 2002 s. 49.
473. Trade Marks Act 2002 s. 50.
474. Trade Marks Act 2002 s. 9.
475. Trade Marks Act 2002 s. 12.
476. Trade Marks Act 2002 s. 82(1).
477. Trade Marks Act 2002 s. 5(1). 'Owner' is defined in relation to a registered collective trade mark as the collective association in whose name the trade mark is registered; and in relation to a registered certification trade mark as the person who certifies the goods or services to which the certification trade mark relates. In relation to an unregistered trade mark, 'owner' means the person who owns all of the rights in the mark.
478. Trade Marks Act 2002 s. 82(2).
479. Trade Marks Act 2002 s. 82(3).

of the trade mark is authorized by, and subject to the control of, the owner of the trade mark.[480] Section 7(2) also refers to licensing in the definition of use of a trade mark. It provides that references in the Act to use of a trade mark by the owner includes use by a person other than the owner if that use is authorized by, and subject to, the control of the owner.

There is also provision for licenses to be assigned or transmitted. Section 85 provides that nothing in the Act prevents a licensee from assigning or transmitting the right to use a trade mark.

§6. Scope of Exclusive Rights

141. Section 10 of the Trade Marks Act 2002 sets out the exclusive rights that attach to registered trade marks. Section 10(1) provides as follows:

> The owner of a registered trade mark has, in relation to all or any of the goods or services in respect of which the trade mark is registered, the rights and remedies provided by this Act and, in particular, has the exclusive right to:

(a) use the registered trade mark; and
(b) authorize other persons to use the registered trade mark; and
(c) assign or transmit the registered trade mark (either in connection with the goodwill of a business or not); and
(d) give valid receipts for any consideration for any such assignment or transmission.

The exclusive rights as set out are subject to any conditions entered on the register in relation to the registered trade mark.[481] The rights accrue from the deemed date of registration of the trade mark, which is generally the date of registration.[482]

There is an additional provision specifying the rights of a collective association in relation to a collective trade mark.[483]

The right to use the trade mark is a core right for owners of registered marks. Section 7 defines 'use' in relation to a trade mark. 'Use' includes use in a form differing in elements that do not alter the distinctive character of the trade mark in the form in which it was registered. It also includes applying the trade mark to goods or services or to labelling or packaging of goods or services in New Zealand for export purposes. 'Use' includes use by the owner and also use by a person other than the owner if that use is authorized by, and subject to, the control of the owner.

480. Trade Marks Act 2002 s. 5(1).
481. Trade Marks Act 2002 s. 11(a). 'Condition' is defined in the Trade Marks Act 2002 s. 5(1).
482. Trade Marks Act 2002 s. 11(b) and s. 5(1).
483. Trade Marks Act 2002 s. 10(2).

§7. Limitations of the Scope of Trade Mark Protection

142. There may be limitations on the scope of protection for an individual trade mark. A trade mark may be registered subject to any conditions the Commissioner thinks fit.[484] 'Condition' includes a limitation of the exclusive right to use a trade mark given by the registration of the trade mark, including a limitation of that right as to mode of use, use in relation to goods to be sold or otherwise traded in any place within New Zealand, use in relation to services to be provided within New Zealand, and use in relation to goods to be exported to any market outside New Zealand.[485]

A trade mark owner may voluntarily disclaim any right to the exclusive use of any part of the trade mark.[486] The Commissioner or the court may also require a disclaimer of any right to the exclusive use of a word or words in relation to any goods or services, as a condition of registration or of not having the trade mark revoked.[487] The Commissioner or the court may also require a disclaimer if it is considered that there are public interest reasons for doing so.[488] A disclaimer may be required where some words or parts of the mark are descriptive or generic.[489]

§8. Use Requirements

143. A registered trade mark may be revoked for non-use. An aggrieved person may apply to the Commissioner or the court for the revocation of the registration of a trade mark on the grounds of non-use.[490]

The registration may be revoked on the grounds that at no time during a continuous period of three years or more was the trade mark put to genuine use in the course of trade in New Zealand, by the owner for the time being, in relation to goods or services in respect of which it is registered.[491] A 'continuous period' means a period that commences from a date after the actual date of registration and continues uninterrupted up to the date one month before the application for revocation.[492] The use must be genuine use, and it must be in the course of trade. The trade mark must not be revoked if use is resumed or commenced before the application for revocation.[493]

A trade mark may not be revoked for non-use if its non-use is due to special circumstances that are outside the control of the owner of the trade mark.[494] If opposing

484. Trade Marks Act 2002 s. 40.
485. Trade Marks Act 2002 s. 5(1).
486. Trade Marks Act 2002 s. 69.
487. Trade Marks Act 2002 s. 70.
488. Trade Marks Act 2002 s. 71.
489. *See* , e.g., the disclaimer required in *Intellectual Reserve Inc v. Robert Sintes* [2009] NZCA 305, (Arnold, Ellen France & Baragwanath JJ).
490. Trade Marks Act 2002 s. 65 and s. 66(1).
491. Trade Marks Act 2002 s. 66(1)(a).
492. Trade Marks Act 2002 s. 66(1A).
493. Trade Marks Act 2002 s. 66(3). However *see also* s. 66(4).
494. Trade Marks Act 2002 s. 66(2). *See Manhaas Industries (2000) Ltd v. Fresha Export Ltd* [2012] NZHC 1815.

revocation, the owner or licensee is required to provide proof of the use of the trade mark or raise the special circumstances that justify the non-use.[495]

Revocation for non-use can be in relation to all use, or can relate to only some of the goods or services in respect of which it is registered.[496] If it is revoked to any extent, the owner's rights cease on the date of application for revocation or an earlier date if the Commissioner or the court is satisfied that grounds for revocation existed at that earlier date.[497]

'Use' is defined in sections 6 and 7. It includes use in a form differing in elements that do not alter the distinctive character of the trade mark in the form in which it was registered.[498] It also includes use by a person authorized by the owner, meaning a licensee.[499]

§9. Duration of Protection, Renewal, Termination

I. Duration and Renewal

144. The duration of registration of a trade mark is effective for ten years from the deemed date of registration (generally the date of application), unless the trade mark ceases to be registered before the expiration of the ten-year period.[500] The trade mark may be renewed for further periods of ten years.[501]

II. Termination

145. Registration of a trade mark may be cancelled voluntarily by the owner in relation to all or any of the goods or services in respect of which it is registered.[502] Registration may also be cancelled or altered by the Commissioner or the court on the ground of failure to comply with a condition of registration.[503] There are additional provisions for cancellation or alteration of certification and collective trade marks.[504]

Registration of a trade mark may be revoked by the Commissioner or the court on the application of an aggrieved person.[505] The grounds for revocation of a trade

495. Trade Marks Act 2002 s. 67.
496. Trade Marks Act 2002 s. 68(1). *See Sky Network Television Ltd v. Skyfiber Inc* [2012] NZHC 3559.
497. Trade Marks Act 2002 s. 68(2).
498. Trade Marks Act 2002 s. 7(1)(a). *See Crocodile International PTE Ltd v. Lacoste* [2016] NZCA 111.
499. Trade Marks Act 2002 s. 7(2).
500. Trade Marks Act 2002 s. 57.
501. Trade Marks Act 2002 ss 58 and 59.
502. Trade Marks Act 2002 s. 61.
503. Trade Marks Act 2002 s. 62.
504. Trade Marks Act 2002 ss 63 and 64.
505. Trade Marks Act 2002 s. 65.

mark are set out in section 66. Section 66 provides that registration may be revoked on the following grounds:

- Non-use for a continuous period of three years or more.[506]
- That the trade mark has become generic.[507] The provision for revocation on grounds of genericism requires that the trade mark must have become a common name in general public use for a product or service in respect of which it is registered, in consequence of acts or inactivity of the owner.[508]
- That the word or words constituting the mark are the only practicable name for an invention that was formerly the subject of a patent, since expired.[509]
- That the trade mark is likely to deceive or confuse the public as a consequence of use by the owner or with the owner's consent in relation to goods or services in respect of which it is registered. This likely deception or confusion may occur, for instance, as to the nature, quality, or geographical origin of those goods or services.[510]

If grounds for revocation exist in respect of only some of the goods or services in respect of which the trade mark is registered, revocation relates only to those goods or services.[511]

The Commissioner or the court may, on the application of an aggrieved person (which includes a person who is culturally aggrieved), declare that the registration of a trade mark is invalid to the extent that the trade mark was not registrable at the deemed date of its registration.[512] Where a trade mark has acquired distinctiveness after registration, it must not be declared invalid even if it was not registrable at the deemed date of its registration.[513] The grounds for invalidity are in Part 2 of the Act, and cover the requirements for a trade mark to be registrable in sections 17, 18 and 25.

§10. Infringement and Remedies

146. The Trade Marks Act 2002 Part 4 covers legal proceedings in relation to trade marks.

Subpart 1 covers civil proceedings for infringement of registered trade marks. Subpart 2 covers criminal proceedings, and subpart 3 covers border protection measures.

---

506. Trade Marks Act 2002 s. 66(1)(a) Non-use has been discussed in §8 under Use requirements.
507. Trade Marks Act 2002 s. 66(1)(c).
508. Trade Marks Act 2002 s. 66(1)(c). This provision received detailed consideration by the New Zealand Court of Appeal in *Tasman Insulation New Zealand Ltd v. Knauf Insulation Ltd* [2015] NZCA 602. In relation to the previous provision in the Trade Marks Act 1953, *see Waitomo Adventures Ltd v. BWR Resources Ltd* High Court, Hamilton, (CP72/00) 26 Apr. 2002, Randerson J.
509. Trade Marks Act 2002 s. 66(1)(d).
510. Trade Marks Act 2002 s. 66(1)(e).
511. Trade Marks Act 2002 s. 68(1).
512. Trade Marks Act 2002 s. 73(1).
513. Trade Marks Act 2002 s. 73(2).

I. Civil Proceedings for Infringement

147. Infringement proceedings for registered trade marks may generally be brought at any time after the deemed date of registration of the mark.[514] There is provision in relation to unjustified proceedings.[515]

Section 89 applies to infringement of a registered trade mark by use of an identical or similar sign in the course of trade. Section 89 provides that a person infringes a registered trade mark if the person does not have the right to use the registered trade mark and uses in the course of trade a sign:

(a) identical with the registered trade mark in relation to any goods or services in respect of which the trade mark is registered; or
(b) identical with the registered trade mark in relation to any goods or services that are similar to any goods or services in respect of which the trade mark is registered, if that use would be likely to deceive or confuse; or
(c) similar to the registered trade mark in relation to any goods or services that are identical with or similar to any goods or services in respect of which the trade mark is registered, if that use would be likely to deceive or confuse; or
(d) identical with or similar to the registered trade mark in relation to any goods or services that are not similar to the goods or services in respect of which the trade mark is registered where the trade mark is well-known in New Zealand and the use of the sign takes unfair advantage of, or is detrimental to, the distinctive character or the repute of the mark.

Section 89(2) requires that the sign is used in the course of trade and in such a manner as to render the use of the sign as likely to be taken as being used as a trade mark.[516] Use of a sign includes use of the sign on or in relation to goods or services, and includes audible use.[517] Section 89(2) was considered in *Intercity Group (NZ) Ltd v. Nakedbus NZ Ltd,*[518] a case involving the use of Google AdWords. Nakedbus used its rival Intercity's mark in AdWords, so that its own advertising was displayed in response to searches for 'Intercity'. The High Court found that, as this use of the mark could not be seen by the consumer, it could not be 'taken as being used as a trade mark' under section 89(2).[519]

148. Section 89(1)(a): The first category of infringement in section 89 is use of an identical sign in relation to goods or services for which the mark is registered. A comparison of signs is required to assess whether they are identical, which may raise issues in marginal cases. Confusion is not required.

514. Trade Marks Act 2002 s. 100.
515. Trade Marks Act 2002 s. 105.
516. Trade Marks Act 2002 s. 89(2).
517. Trade Marks Act 2002 s. 6.
518. *Intercity Group (NZ) Ltd v. Nakedbus NZ Ltd* [2014] 3 NZLR 177.
519. *Intercity Group (NZ) Ltd v. Nakedbus NZ Ltd* [2014] 3 NZLR 177, 195. This approach was approved by the Court of Appeal in *Tasman Insulation New Zealand Ltd v. Knauf Insulation Ltd* [2015] NZCA 602.

149. Section 89(1)(b): The second category is use of an identical sign in relation to any goods or services that are similar to goods or services in respect of which the trade mark is registered, if that use would be likely to deceive or confuse.

Here the sign has to be identical, but the goods and services only have to be similar. New Zealand courts have followed the approach taken in *British Sugar PLC v. James Robertson & Sons Ltd.*[520] In that case, the Judge was required to consider whether the two marks were used for similar goods. The Judge noted that the wider the scope of the concept, the wider the absolute scope of protection of a mark. He said that, in effect, a registration covers the goods of the specification plus similar goods. No one may use the registered mark or a similar mark for any of those goods unless he has some other defence. This suggested a need for caution, as otherwise, however narrow a specification, the actual protection will be wide. The Judge said that the following factors must be relevant in considering whether there is or is not similarity of goods:

(a) The respective uses of the respective goods or services.
(b) The respective users of the respective goods or services.
(c) The physical nature of the goods or acts of service.
(d) The respective trade channels through which the goods or services reach the market.
(e) In the case of self-serve consumer items, where in practice they are respectively found or likely to be found in supermarkets and in particular whether they are, or are likely to be, found on the same or different shelves.
(f) The extent to which the respective goods or services are competitive. This inquiry may take into account how those in trade classify goods, for instance whether market research companies, who of course act for industry, put the goods or services in the same or different sectors.

This category requires that the goods or services be similar, and that use of the sign would be likely to deceive or confuse. Generally, this means confusion or deception of a substantial number of persons as to the trade origin of the goods or services.[521] Evidence of actual confusion is not required and confusion can be post-sale.[522]

150. Section 89(1)(c): The third category is use in the course of trade of a similar sign in relation to any goods or services that are identical with or similar to any goods or services in respect of which the trade mark is registered, if that use would be likely to deceive or confuse. This applies where the signs are similar rather than identical, and where the goods or services are identical or similar. Likelihood of deception or confusion is required.

520. 1996 R.P.C. 281 (Ch). The approach taken in this case has been applied in New Zealand. *See* , e.g., *NV Sumatra Tobacco Trading Co v. New Zealand Milk Brands Ltd* [2011] 3 NZLR 206 (CA).

521. *See Pioneer Hi-Bred Corn Co v. Hy-Line Chicks Pty Ltd* [1978] 2 NZLR 50 (CA), *Mainland Products Ltd v. Bonlac Foods (NZ) Ltd* [1998] 3 NZLR 341 (CA) *Levi Strauss & Co v. Kimbyr Investments Ltd* [1994] 1 NZLR 332 (HC).

522. *Levi Strauss & Co v. Kimbyr Investments Ltd* [1994] 1 NZLR 332 (HC).

The marks must be similar enough to deceive or confuse. The plaintiffs' mark as registered must be compared with the defendant's mark as it appears in actual use.[523] The test from *Re Pianotist Co's Application*[524] is applied by New Zealand courts. This case sets out the established test for comparing trade marks in order to determine whether they are similar. Parker J said:

> You must take the two words. You must judge of them, both by their look and by their sound. You must consider the nature and kind of customer who would be likely to buy those goods. In fact, you must consider all the surrounding circumstances; and you must further consider what is likely to happen if each of those trade marks is used in a normal way as a trade mark for the goods of the respective owners of the marks.

The imperfect recollection of the ordinary customer must be borne in mind. The 'idea of the mark' must be carefully considered, and consideration must also be given to all the circumstances of the trade in which the marks in question are employed.[525]

There must also be likely deception or confusion, as discussed above.

151. Section 89(1)(d): The fourth category is the anti-dilution provision in section 89(1)(d), which is entirely new in the 2002 Act. This category is use in the course of trade of a sign that is identical or similar to the registered trade mark. It covers use of the identical or similar sign in relation to non-similar goods or services where the trade mark is well known in New Zealand and the use of the sign takes unfair advantage of, or is detrimental to, the distinctive character or the repute of the mark.

This provision gives additional protection to the category of marks that are 'well known in New Zealand'. There is little New Zealand case law as yet on what constitutes 'well known in New Zealand'.[526] The term is not defined, and there are issues still to be resolved such as to the extent of reputation required, whether it equates to 'famous' in other jurisdictions. These issues also arise in relation to section 25(1)(c).

Where a mark is well known in New Zealand, the provision applies to use of an identical or similar sign in relation to non-similar goods or services where the use of the sign takes unfair advantage of, or is detrimental to, the distinctive character or the repute of the mark. These terms are not defined in the Act, and case law has not yet provided clear approaches. Likelihood of confusion is not a requirement in the provision, and dilution occurs in the absence of confusion. Taking unfair advantage can nevertheless potentially involve a link in the minds of consumers between the plaintiff's mark and the defendant's use of an identical or similar mark. Detriment to the distinctive character or repute of the mark involves the concepts of tarnishment of the mark and blurring

523. *See Levi Strauss & Co v. Kimbyr Investments Ltd* [1994] 1 NZLR 332 (HC).
524. (1906) 23 RPC 774 at 777.
525. *See Levi Strauss & Co v. Kimbyr Investments Ltd* [1994] 1 NZLR 332 (HC).
526. It was accepted that Milk Brands' ANCHOR mark was well known in New Zealand for dairy products in *NV Sumatra Tobacco Trading Co v. New Zealand Milk Brands Ltd* [2011] NZCA 264; [2011] 3 NZLR 206.

of distinctiveness. Precisely how these concepts apply in the New Zealand context has yet to be resolved.[527]

152. Section 90: Section 90 is an additional infringement provision. It provides that infringement will occur where there is a contract between the registered trade mark owner or licensee and the purchaser or owner of goods not to do certain listed acts in relation to the trade mark and the owner or purchaser of the goods does those listed acts.[528] The listed acts include applying the trade mark to the goods after they have been altered, altering the trade mark on the goods and applying another trade mark to the goods.[529]

153. Defences: The infringement provisions in section 89 are subject to the defences in sections 92–98.

154. There is no defence arising from use of the name under which a company is registered.[530]

155. There is a defence for use of a trade mark in any way or in any circumstances to which the registration does not extend, having regard to any conditions entered on the register in relation to the trade mark.[531] A registered trade mark is also is not infringed by the use of another registered trade mark in relation to any goods or services for which that other trade mark is registered.[532]

156. The 2002 Act contains a new defence for comparative advertising. Under previous legislation, use of a trade mark for purposes of comparative advertising constituted an infringement.[533] Section 94 now provides that a registered trade mark is not infringed by the use of the registered trade mark for the purposes of comparative advertising, but any such use otherwise than in accordance with honest practices in industrial or commercial matters must be treated as infringing the registered trade mark if the use, without due cause, takes unfair advantage of, or is detrimental to, the distinctive character or the repute of the trade mark.[534] There are issues of interpretation still to be dealt with by the New Zealand courts, particularly as to the meaning of 'honest practices in industrial or commercial matters',[535] and 'without due cause, takes unfair advantage of, or is detrimental to, the distinctive character or the repute of the trade mark'.

157. Section 95 provides a defence for a person doing certain listed acts if done in accordance with honest practices in industrial and commercial matters. The listed acts include the use of the person's name or the name of the person's place of business,[536] use of the name of the person's predecessor in business or the name of the person's

---

527. *See* discussion in Paul Sumpter, *Trade Marks in Practice* 178–183 (3rd ed., LexisNexis N.Z. Ltd. 2015).
528. Trade Marks Act 2002 s. 90.
529. Trade Marks Act 2002 s. 90(2).
530. Trade Marks Act 2002 s. 91.
531. Trade Marks Act 2002 s. 92.
532. Trade Marks Act 2002 s. 93.
533. *PC Direct v. Best Buys* [1997] 2 NZLR 723 (HC).
534. Trade Marks Act 2002 s. 94.
535. Courts are likely to use the approach in *Cable and Wireless v. BT* [1998] FSR 383, 389. *See also Benchmark Building Supplies Limited v. Mitre 10 NZ Ltd* [2004] 1 NZLR 26 (CA).
536. Trade Marks Act 2002 s. 95(a).

predecessor's place of business,[537] use of a sign to indicate characteristics or time of production or rendering of goods or services,[538] and use of the trade mark where reasonably necessary to indicate the intended purpose of the goods (in particular as accessories or spare parts) or services.[539]

158. Section 96 provides a defence where there has been prior continuous use of the identical or a similar unregistered mark by someone else before the date of application or use of the registered mark. The defence applies in relation to identical or similar goods and services.[540]

159. Sections 97, 97A and 98 provide a defence for genuine use of a mark where the mark has been applied by or with the consent of the owner. These sections generally prevent trade mark infringement actions in cases of parallel importation. Section 98 provides for deemed consent in relation to imported medicines.

160. Remedies: Relief available for infringement of registered trade marks includes injunctions and either damages or account of profits.[541] Interim injunctions are available. There is provision for orders to erase, remove or obliterate an offending sign or to destroy infringing goods, material or objects.[542] The court may also order delivery up of infringing goods, material or objects.[543]

161. Criminal proceedings: The Trade Marks Act 2002 Part 4 Subpart 2 provides for criminal proceedings. It creates a number of offences, and there is provision for a body corporate to be convicted, in which case every director and manager is guilty of the offence if it is proved that the act took place with his or her authority, permission or consent and that he or she knew or could reasonably be expected to have known that the offence was to be or was being committed and failed to take all reasonable steps to prevent or stop it.[544]

Offences created by the Act are the following:

- Counterfeiting a registered trade mark with the intention of obtaining a gain or causing a loss to any person.[545] A person counterfeits a registered trade mark if, without the consent of the owner of the registered trade mark, the person knowingly makes a sign that is identical to, or similar to, the registered trade mark so as to be likely to deceive; or falsifies a genuine registered trade mark, whether by alteration, addition, effacement, partial removal or otherwise.[546]
- Falsely applying a registered trade mark to goods or services.[547] A person falsely applies a registered trade mark to goods or services if the person knowingly applies the trade mark or a sign that the person knows is likely to be mistaken

537. Trade Marks Act 2002 s. 95(b).
538. Trade Marks Act 2002 s. 95(c).
539. Trade Marks Act 2002 s. 95(d).
540. Trade Marks Act 2002 s. 96.
541. Trade Marks Act 2002 s. 106.
542. Trade Marks Act 2002 s. 108.
543. Trade Marks Act 2002 ss 109–116.
544. Trade Marks Act 2002 s. 119.
545. Trade Marks Act 2002 s. 120(1).
546. Trade Marks Act 2002 s. 120(2).
547. Trade Marks Act 2002 s. 121(1).

for that trade mark to the goods or services without the consent of the owner of the registered trade mark and in the case of goods, knows the goods are not the genuine goods of the owner or licensee of the registered trade mark.[548] There are broad definitions for applying a trade mark or sign.[549]

- Making an object specifically designed or adapted for making copies of a registered trade mark or a sign that is likely to be mistaken for a trade mark with intent that the object be used for, or in the course of, committing an offence against section 120 or section 121.[550]
- Possessing an object specifically designed or adapted for making copies of a registered trade mark or a sign that is likely to be mistaken for a trade mark with intent that the object be used for or in course of committing an offence under section 120 or section 121.[551]
- Importing goods for the purpose of trade or manufacture knowing that a registered trade mark has been falsely applied to those goods, or selling or exposing for sale or possessing for the purpose of trade or manufacture goods to which the person knows a registered trade mark is falsely applied.[552]

162. Penalties and remedies: Penalties are provided for in section 125. This provides for fines up to New Zealand Dollar (NZD) 10,000 for each of the goods or services to which the offence relates but not exceeding NZD 150,000 for the same transaction, or imprisonment for a term not exceeding five years.

Orders for delivery up or disposal are also available in criminal proceedings.[553] The criminal enforcement provisions of the Trade Marks Act have recently been strengthened. The Trade Marks Amendment Act 2011 introduced provisions for the Ministry of Economic Development to appoint Enforcement Officers with powers of search and seizure, with and without search warrants.[554] The functions of Enforcement Officers are to gather information relating to offences under the Act, investigate offences under the Act, and report on any matters relating to the enforcement Officer's functions.[555]

The Act also provides for border protection measures and powers of search and seizure for the New Zealand Customs Service.[556]

§11. Overlapping and Relation to Other Intellectual Property Laws

163. There is significant overlap between trade mark law and copyright law and trade mark law and designs law. Some trade marks, particularly signs such as logos

548. Trade Marks Act 2002 s. 121(2).
549. Trade Marks Act 2002 s. 121(3)-(5).
550. Trade Marks Act 2002 s. 122.
551. Trade Marks Act 2002 s. 123.
552. Trade Marks Act 2002 s. 124.
553. Trade Marks Act 2002 ss 126–128.
554. Trade Marks Act 2002 Part 4 Subpart 2A.
555. Trade Marks Act 2002 s. 134C.
556. Trade Marks Act 2002 Part 4 Subpart 3.

and combinations of signs, will also constitute copyright works and be protected by copyright. Some trade marks, may also be registrable as industrial designs.[557] There is also overlap between the protection of trade marks as described and the protection provided under the Major Events Management Act 2007 which provides protection for major international events that are held in New Zealand, protecting against ambush marketing by association and intrusion.

However, the most significant overlap is between the protection provided under the Trade Marks Act 2002 for registered trade marks and the protection provided to unregistered trade marks by common law and consumer protection statute law.

164. Unregistered trade marks: Unregistered trade marks are protected by the common law tort of passing off and under the statutory protection against misleading and deceptive conduct in trade in the Fair Trading Act 1986.[558] Section 88 of the Trade Marks Act 2002 provides that these causes of action are not affected by the Trade Marks Act.

165. The tort of passing off can be used to protect unregistered trade marks. A plaintiff needs to show that there is some reputation or goodwill attached to its name, mark or get-up, that the defendant has used the same or a deceptively similar name, mark or get-up so as to confuse or deceive the relevant public or if unrestrained is likely to do so, and that as a result damage has been or is likely to plaintiff's business.[559] However, passing off has an important limitation in that it cannot be used to protect functional features.[560]

166. The Fair Trading Act 1986 is consumer protection legislation. It can be used by traders against misleading or deceptive conduct by other traders, in a similar way to passing off protection.

167 The Fair Trading Act 1986 section 9 provides that:

> No person shall, in trade,[561] engage in conduct that is misleading or deceptive or is likely to mislead or deceive.

In a passing off type action to protect an unregistered trade mark based on section 9 of the Fair Trading Act 1986, a plaintiff would have to prove that:[562]

(i) the goods or services in question have an existing reputation which in the minds of customers is associated with a particular name, mark or get-up;

(ii) the defendant's conduct was committed in a trade context; and

557. Designs Act 1953.
558. Trade Marks Act 2002 s. 88.
559. *Tot Toys Ltd v. Mitchell* [1993] 1 NZLR 325, 334 (HC).
560. *Tot Toys Ltd v. Mitchell* [1993] 1 NZLR 325, (HC).
561. Fair Trading Act 1986 s. 2 (1) 'Trade' means any trade, business, industry, profession, occupation, activity of commerce, or undertaking relating to the supply or acquisition of goods or services or to the disposition or acquisition of any interest in land.
562. *Tot Toys Ltd v. Mitchell* [1993] 1 NZLR 325, 367(HC).

(iii) that conduct caused or is likely to cause customers to be misled or deceived over the implications of that name, mark or get-up.

The requirements of the Fair Trading Act section 9 action are easier to meet than are the requirements for passing off.[563] There is no need to prove damage or source motivation, and no need for plaintiff to be owner of the reputation with which the defendant is being confused. Deception at any time constitutes a breach, and there is no distinction between functional and other features. However, while it is easier to establish the cause of action, the remedies under the Fair Trading Act are discretionary, and the court's dominant consideration is the interests of consumers. In exceptional cases, a remedy may be denied on the ground that the deception would have no real impact upon consumers and/or that an injunction would be contrary to their interests.[564]

Commonly actions are brought in both passing off and under section 9 of the Fair Trading Act in New Zealand. However, as with trade marks law, protection is limited to protection against misrepresentations.

563. *Tot Toys Ltd v. Mitchell* [1993] 1 NZLR 325, 367–368 (HC).
564. *Tot Toys Ltd v. Mitchell* [1993] 1 NZLR 325, 371 (HC).

Chapter 5. Tradenames

168. New Zealand law does not operate a separate system for the protection of tradenames, and there is no separate register. It generally protects tradenames in the same way as other trade marks. Generally, tradenames that are registered trade marks are protected under the Trade Marks Act 2002, and if unregistered can be protected by the common law or under the Fair Trading Act 1986.[565]

169. The Companies Act 1993 does however provide some limited protection for company names. Section 22 of the Companies Act 1993 applies to applications for reservation of a company name. It provides for applications for reservation of a name to be sent to the Registrar of Companies,[566] and provides that:[567]

The Registrar must not reserve a name—

(a) the use of which would contravene an enactment; or
(b) that is identical or almost identical to the name of another company; or
(c) that is identical or almost identical to a name that the Registrar has already reserved under this Act and that is still available for registration; or
(d) that, in the opinion of the Registrar, is offensive.

This offers only limited protection however. The courts focus on the efficiency of the registration process and generally leave the protection of trade names to the regimes designed for that purpose, that is, the Trade Marks Act, passing off and the Fair Trading Act.[568]

565. *See* , e.g., *Neumegen v. Neumegen and Co* [1998] 3 NZLR 310 (CA).
566. Companies Act 1993 s. 22(1).
567. Companies Act 1993 s. 22(2).
568. *See New Zealand Conference of Seventh-Day Adventists v. Registrar of Companies* [1997] 1 NZLR 751. (HC), *Dr Rust Ltd v. Registrar of Companies* (1997) 8 NZCLC 261, 501.

Chapter 6. Industrial Designs

170. Industrial designs receive protection from more than one regime in New Zealand law. New Zealand has a regime of registered design protection, under the Designs Act 1953. Copyright protection is also available for designs, which are protected as artistic works. Industrial designs are not excluded from copyright protection although there is a reduced term of protection for artistic works applied industrially. Design registration under the Designs Act 1953 requires application and the payment of fees, making it less attractive than copyright.

Copyright protection has been covered in Chapter 1 and trade marks law in Chapter 4. This chapter deals with designs protection under the Designs Act 1953.

§1. Sources: Legislation

171. The Designs Act 1953 and Designs Regulations 1954 provide a regime for registered design protection.

The Copyright Act 1994 also provides protection for designs.

The Trade Marks Act 2002 can also be used to protect designs if these are used as trade marks.

The tort of passing off and the Fair Trading Act 1986 can also be used to protect designs where these are used as unregistered trade marks.

§2. Subject Matter of Protection

172. Protection is available for designs, as defined in the Designs Act 1953 which provides:[569]

> Design means features of shape, configuration, pattern, or ornament applied to an article by any industrial process or means, being features which in the finished article appeal to and are judged solely by the eye; but does not include a method or principle of construction or features of shape or configuration which are dictated solely by the function which the article to be made in that shape or configuration has to perform.

Registered designs protection therefore applies to features of external appearance of an article, features of shape, configuration, pattern or ornamentation. Pattern and ornamentation generally covers two-dimensional features, and shape and configuration covers three-dimensional features. Purely functional aspects are not protected by registered design protection, unless they contribute to external appearance.

173. The features of shape, configuration, pattern or ornamentation must be applied to an article, and 'article' is separately defined:[570]

569. Designs Act 1953 (NZ) s. 2.
570. Designs Act 1953 (NZ) s. 2.

> Article means any article of manufacture; and includes any part of an article if that part is made and sold separately.

The article must have some function other than having the design applied to it.[571] To be registrable, a design must involve features of shape, configuration, pattern or ornament, appealing to and judged solely by the eye, not being a method or principle of construction or features dictated solely by function.[572] The features of appearance must have eye appeal in the sense that they appeal to and are judged by the eye of the prospective customer in making a selection.[573]

174. Some designs are excluded from registration under the Designs Regulations 1954, because of the category of articles to which they are applied, particularly where the article operates merely as a vehicle for the design. Regulation 33 provides:[574]

> There shall be excluded from registration under the Act designs to be applied to any of the following articles, namely:

(a) Works of sculpture other than casts or models used or intended to be used as models or patterns to be multiplied by any industrial process:
(b) Wall plaques and medals:
(c) Printed matter primarily of a literary or artistic character, including bookjackets, calendars, certificates, coupons, dressmaking patterns, greetings cards, leaflets, maps, plans, postcards, stamps, trade advertisements, trade forms, and cards, transfers, and the like.

§3. Conditions of Protection

175. The design must be new or original.[575] Novelty in the registered designs regime means local novelty, in the sense that the design is new if it has not been made available to the public in New Zealand before the application date.[576] Section 5(2) provides that:

> a design shall not be registered thereunder unless it is new or original and in particular shall not be so registered in respect of any article if it is the same as a design which before the date of the application for registration has been registered or published in New Zealand in respect of the same or any other article or differs

571. Littlewoods Pools Ltd's Application (1949) 66 RPC 309. *See also* discussion in James & Wells Intellectual Property Law in New Zealand 275–276 (Ian Finch ed., Brookers Ltd. 2007).
572. The provision that 'design' does not include a method or principle of construction or features of shape or configuration which are dictated solely by the function which the article to be made in that shape or configuration has to perform has caused some difficulty for the courts. *See Interlego AG v. Tyco Industries Inc* [1989] 1 AC 217 (PC).
573. *AMP v. Utilux Pty Ltd* (1972) 89 RPC 103 (HL) 108–109.
574. Designs Regulations 1954, Regulation 33.
575. Designs Act 1953 (NZ) s. 5(2).
576. Designs Act 1953 (NZ) s. 5(2).

from such a design only in immaterial details or in features which are variants commonly used in the trade.

Although novelty is a local novelty standard, the standard of novelty is nevertheless higher than that in copyright law. It is not enough that the design originates from the author; it must actually qualify as novel, as being 'new or original'. The term 'new or original' is not separately defined in the Act.[577] However, it is clear from the section that a design is not novel if it is the same as a design registered or published in New Zealand before the date of application. Prior registration or publication destroys novelty even if it has been applied in the past to another article, not the article for which registration is sought. The prior art design need not be identical, it will still destroy novelty if it differs from the design only in immaterial details or in features which are variants commonly used in the trade. A design application must include a statement of novelty, which sets out the features in which novelty is claimed.

§4. Formalities (Procedure for Grant and Obtaining Protection)

176. The formalities for obtaining protection are set out in the Designs Act 1953[578] and the Designs Regulations 1954. Applicants for design registration are required to provide a signed application form with fee, representations of the design and a statement of novelty.[579]

On receipt of an application, the IPONZ will examine for registrability,[580] and either issue a Certificate of Registration or an examination report stating objections. There is provision for hearings and for appeal from the IPONZ decision.[581]

§5. Ownership and Transfer

177. The author is generally the proprietor of the registered design.[582] However where a design is commissioned, the commissioner is the proprietor.[583] A registered design may be assigned, transmitted, transferred by operation of law or licensed.[584] These are required to be registered.[585]

577. The term was considered in *Bruce Sutton and Anor v. Bay Masonry Ltd and Anor.* (High Court Tauranga, CIV 2003 470 000260, 28 May 2004, Williams J).
578. Designs Act 1953 s. 7.
579. *See* Designs Regulations 1954 Parts 5 and 6, Intellectual Property Office of New Zealand *Registered Design Protection* 1 Aug. 2002. *See* http://www.iponz.govt.nz/cms/designs (accessed 9 Apr. 2014), Intellectual Property Office of New Zealand *The Designs Process*, 2012, http://www.iponz.govt.nz/cms/designs/the-designs-process (accessed 9 Apr. 2014).
580. Designs Regulations 1954 Part 8.
581. Designs Regulations 1954 ss 36–38.
582. Designs Act 1953 s. 6.
583. Designs Act 1953 s. 6(1).
584. Designs Act 1953 s. 6(2).
585. Designs Act 1953 s. 27, Designs Regulations 1954 s. 45.

§6. Scope of Exclusive Rights

178. Registration of a design gives the owner of the design exclusive rights broader than those provided by copyright. The Designs Act 1953 provides that registration gives to the registered proprietor:[586]

> the exclusive right in New Zealand to make or import for sale or for use for the purposes of any trade or business, or to sell, hire, or offer for sale or hire, any article in respect of which the design is registered, being an article to which the registered design or a design not substantially different from the registered design has been applied, and to make anything for enabling any such article to be made as aforesaid, whether in New Zealand or elsewhere.

A registered design therefore gives the proprietor exclusive rights to make, import, sell or offer to sell and hire or offer to hire, and these rights cover not only protection against copying but also protection against independent creation of the same or not a substantially similar design in relation to any article in respect of which the design is registered. Design registration also prevents imports of the design, including parallel imports.

§7. Limitations of the Scope of Protection

179. The design protected is that described in the statement of novelty. Protection of features not set out in the statement of novelty is excluded.[587] Purely functional aspects are not protected by registered design protection, unless they contribute to external appearance.

§8. Duration of Protection

180. Design protection lasts for a term of fifteen years in total. A design is initially registered for five years.[588] It may be renewed for a second or third period of five years.[589]

§9. Infringement and Remedies

181. A registered design is infringed when the article alleged to be an infringement has substantially the same appearance as the registered design.[590] This involves a

---

586. Designs Act 1953 (NZ) s. 11.
587. *See Brand Developers Ltd v. Ezibuy Ltd* (High Court, Auckland, CIV-2010-404-007593, 4 Feb. 2011, Asher J.) [25]-[26].
588. Designs Regulations 1954 Part 9.
589. Designs Act 1953 (NZ) s. 12.
590. *UPL Group Ltd v. Dux Engineers Ltd* [1989] 3 NZLR 135 (CA).

comparison of the alleged infringement with the registered design.[591] Courts may also apply an imperfect recollection test.[592]

182. Defences to infringement are limited generally to challenging the validity of the design registration or claiming no infringement.[593]

183. Remedies include permanent and interim injunctions, delivery up, and damages or account of profits. Commonly plaintiffs seek an interim injunction on a serious question to be tried basis, and challenges to validity are rarely strong enough at this stage to persuade the court against issuing an interim injunction.[594]

Section 13 provides that damages or account of profits shall not be awarded against innocent infringers, that is, where a defendant proves that at the date of the infringement he or she was not aware and had no reasonable ground for supposing that the design was registered in New Zealand.[595]

§10. Overlapping and Relation to Other Intellectual Property Laws

184. There is overlap between registered design protection, copyright and the laws protecting trade marks. Most designers rely on copyright protection, which is available for all industrial designs. Any design based on drawings obtains automatic copyright protection, irrespective of its functional or utilitarian character. Copyright protects artistic works, particularly drawings and models, and includes designs with no artistic quality, and designs that are purely functional or for purely functional objects.[596] Functional designs are not excluded from copyright, and copyright law is routinely used in New Zealand to protect entirely or partly functional designs and industrial objects, relying particularly on underlying drawings and plans, and prototypes as model.[597] Items such as toys, clothing, packaging, confectionery, industrial devices and machinery are all protected by copyright.

New Zealand has no other unregistered design right because copyright protection is available. Concurrent protection under copyright and registered designs law is available.

In addition, designers may rely on registered trade mark protection under the Trade Marks Act 2002, or unregistered protection relying on the tort of passing off and/or the Fair Trading Act 1986.

---

591. *See* discussion in *James & Wells Intellectual Property Law in New Zealand* 395–396 (2d, Ian Finch ed., Brookers Ltd. 2012).

592. *UPL Group Ltd v. Dux Engineers Ltd* [1989] 3 NZLR 135 (CA).

593. *Bruce Sutton and Anor v. Bay Masonry Ltd and Anor.* (High Court Tauranga, CIV 2003 470 000260, 28 May 2004, Williams J) is an example.

594. *See* discussion in Clive Elliot, *Form Over Function: A Review of Recent Developments in Designs Law*, 62 Intell. Prop. Forum 10, 13–14 (2005).

595. Designs Act 1953 s. 13(1).

596. New Zealand followed United Kingdom authority in this. *See Dorling v. Honnor Marine* [1964] RPC 160.

597. *See AHI Operations v. New Lynn Metalcraft Ltd (No 1) (1982)* 1 NZIPR 381 (HC), *Beckmann v. Mayceys Confectionary Ltd* (1995) 33 IPR 543 (CA), *Lakeland Steel v. Stevens* [1996] 2 NZLR 749.

Chapter 7. Plant Variety Protection

§1. Sources: Legislation

185. Plant varieties are protected in New Zealand law by the Plant Variety Rights Act 1987, which is accompanied by the Plant Variety Rights Regulations 1988. Before the coming into force of the Patents Act 2013, patent protection was also available for plant varieties in New Zealand, but plant varieties were expressly excluded from protection under the new Patents Act.[598]

New Zealand is a party to the International Union for the Protection of New Varieties of Plants (UPOV). New Zealand became a member in 1981 and is a member of the 1978 Act.[599] Members of UPOV adhere to the 1978 Convention or the current 1991 Convention.

The Plant Variety Rights Act 1987 and Regulations provide for the grant and administration of Plant Variety Rights, including establishing and maintaining a plant variety rights register and enforcement of rights.

In 2002, a Review of the Plant Variety Rights Act was undertaken.[600] A draft bill, the Plant Variety Rights Amendment Bill, was put out for consultation but is currently on hold.[601]

§2. Subject Matter of Protection

186. Plant variety rights are available under the Plant Variety Rights Act 1987 for new varieties of plants, providing rights for plant breeders in New Zealand.

'Plant' is defined in the Act to include a fungus, but does not include an alga or bacterium.[602] 'Variety' is defined in the Act to mean a cultivar, or cultivated variety, of a plant, and includes any clone, hybrid, stock, or line, of a plant; but does not include a botanical variety of a plant.[603]

Plant variety rights are therefore available for any plant variety except algae or bacteria, so long as the requirements for grant of a right are met.

598. Patents Act 2013 s. 16.

599. *See Members Of The International Union For The Protection Of New Varieties Of Plants*, http://www.upov.int/export/sites/upov/members/en/pdf/pub423.pdf (accessed 9 Apr. 2014).

600. *See Ministry of Economic Development documents*, http://www.med.govt.nz/business/intellectual-property/plant-variety-rights/review-of-the-plant-variety-rights-act-1987 (accessed 9 Apr. 2014).

601. Plant Variety Rights Amendment Bill, *Draft for Consultation*, http://www.med.govt.nz/business/intellectual-property/pdf-docs-library/plant-variety-rights/draft-pvra-bill-pdf (accessed 9 Apr. 2014).

602. Plant Variety Rights Act 1987 s. 2.

603. Plant Variety Rights Act 1987 s. 2.

§3. Conditions of Protection

187. The Plant Variety Rights Act 1987 provides for the Commissioner of Plant Variety Rights to grant plant variety rights in respect of eligible applications made under the Act. An application will be eligible for making a grant if:[604]

- the applicant has given the Commissioner all reproductive material[605] of the variety concerned that has been requested by the Commissioner;
- The Commissioner has approved for that variety a denomination (a variety name) proposed by the applicant;
- The Commissioner is satisfied that the applicant is an owner of that variety;
- The Commissioner has received the prescribed fee;
- The Commissioner is satisfied that the variety is new, distinct, homogeneous and stable.

I. Denomination

188. To be eligible for a grant in respect of a variety, the applicant must propose a denomination for the new variety. A denomination is the distinguishing name or identification approved for that variety.[606] The proposed denomination must conform with international usage relating to the names of cultivated plants.[607] The denomination needs to be approved by the Commissioner. The name cannot be directly descriptive of any characteristic of the new variety.[608]

The denomination cannot be registered as a trade mark, and a registered trade mark cannot be the denomination.[609] Any person who sells reproductive material of the variety is required to use its denomination and not to associate any trade mark with it unless the denomination is clearly recognizable.[610]

II. New

189. A variety is required to be new to be eligible for a grant of rights. A variety is new if there has been no sale of that variety with the agreement of any relevant owner of that variety in New Zealand, for more than twelve months before the date

604. Plant Variety Rights Act 1987 s. 10(2).
605. 'Reproductive material' is defined in relation to any variety, as meaning 'any portion of a plant of that variety by means of which plants of that variety may be reproduced or propagated; and includes spores, seeds, and whole plants'. Plant Variety Rights Act 1987 s. 2.
606. Plant Variety Rights Act 1987 s. 2.
607. Plant Variety Rights Regulations 1988 (SR 1988/101) cl. 7.
608. *See* discussion in IPONZ, *Trade Marks and Plant Variety Names*, http://www.iponz.govt.nz/cms/pvr/technical-notes-guidelines/trade-marks-and-plant-variety-names (accessed 9 Apr. 2014).
609. IPONZ, *Trade Marks and Plant Variety Names*, http://www.iponz.govt.nz/cms/pvr/technical-notes-guidelines/trade-marks-and-plant-variety-names (accessed 9 Apr. 2014).
610. Plant Variety Rights Act 1987 s. 22.

on which that application was made; and overseas, for more than six years before that date in the case of a woody plant, or for more than four years before that date in every other case.[611]

The above rules about prior sales do not apply to sales made to or by the owner to increase the stock of a variety or for evaluation trials or tests of a variety.[612] A variety also does not cease to be new as a result of sale of material that is not reproductive material or of disposal for purposes other than reproduction of surplus reproductive material produced during breeding, increase of stock, tests or trials.[613]

III. Distinct

190. A variety is required to be distinct to be eligible for a grant of rights. A variety is distinct if it is distinguishable by one or more characteristics from any other variety whose existence was a matter of common knowledge when the application concerned was made.[614] The characteristics by which a variety may be distinguished from others may be morphological, physiological, or of any other kind or description, so long as those characteristics are capable of precise description and recognition.[615]

IV. Homogeneous

191. A variety is required to be homogenous to be eligible for a grant of rights. In determining whether a variety is homogeneous, the Commissioner shall have regard to the particular features of its sexual reproduction or vegetative propagation, as applicable.[616]

V. Stable

192. A variety is required to be stable to be eligible for a grant of rights. A variety is stable if, in its essential characteristics, it remains true to its description after repeated propagation or reproduction. Where the applicant concerned has described particular cycles of reproduction or multiplication for that variety, it is required to remain true to its description at the end of each such cycle.[617]

611. Plant Variety Rights Act 1987 s. 10(4)(a).
612. Plant Variety Rights Act 1987 s. 10(6).
613. Plant Variety Rights Act 1987 s. 10(7).
614. Plant Variety Rights Act 1987 s. 10(4)(b).
615. Plant Variety Rights Act 1987 s. 10(8).
616. Plant Variety Rights Act 1987 s. 10(5).
617. Plant Variety Rights Act 1987 s. 10(4)(c).

§4. Formalities (Procedure for Grant and Obtaining Protection)

193. The formalities for grant of a right are set out in the Plant Variety Rights Act 1987 and regulations.[618] An application is required for a plant variety, to be on the form prescribed.[619] The application requirements vary slightly by the variety involved. Applications are required to be accompanied by a quantity of seed if required in respect of the kind of variety, the prescribed fee and a technical questionnaire in respect to the relevant botanical taxon.[620] Colour photographs may also be required.[621]

The Commissioner may require a description of the origin and breeding and botanical features of the variety concerned, and a description of the aspects of the variety that make it distinctive.[622] A proposed denomination will also be required,[623] as will the prescribed trial or examination fee.[624] The Commissioner may request reproductive material and any other information.[625]

If the Commissioner has insufficient information to be satisfied that a variety is distinct, homogeneous or stable, the Commissioner may undertake or commission, or approve the applicant's undertaking or commissioning of, growing trials of the variety, or may examine and evaluate the results of growing trials already conducted by a person or body independent of the applicant.[626]

There is provision for applications where there is an earlier overseas application for the same variety, where the overseas application is made in a 'convention party' as defined.[627] Generally, this means a member of UPOV, but other entities may be declared to be convention parties.[628]

Once the Commissioner is satisfied that the application complies with the requirements outlined above, details of the application are published in the *Plant Variety Rights Journal*,[629] and made available for inspection in Plant Variety Rights Office.[630] There is then a three-month period in which any person may object on the grounds that the application does not meet the requirements or that the applicant is not the owner of the variety.[631] The objector and applicant are then entitled to be heard before the Commissioner makes a determination.[632] Objections can also be made at any time after grant on the grounds that the variety is not new, distinct, stable and

618. *See also* discussion in *James & Wells Intellectual Property Law in New Zealand* 210–214 (Ian Finch 2ed., Brookers Ltd. 2012).
619. Plant Variety Rights Act 1987 s. 5(1).
620. Plant Variety Rights Act 1987 s. 5(1)(a).
621. Plant Variety Rights Act 1987 s. 5(1)(a)(iii).
622. Plant Variety Rights Act 1987 s. 5(2)(a).
623. Plant Variety Rights Act 1987 s. 5(2)(b).
624. Plant Variety Rights Act 1987 s. 5(2)(c).
625. Plant Variety Rights Act 1987 s. 5(3).
626. Plant Variety Rights Regulations 1988 (SR 1988/101) cl. 16.
627. Plant Variety Rights Act 1987 s. 2.
628. Plant Variety Rights Act 1987 s. 38A.
629. Plant Variety Rights Act 1987 s. 34.
630. Plant Variety Rights Act 1987 s. 8. The Plant Variety Rights Office is provided for in Part 3 of the Plant Variety Rights Act 1987.
631. Plant Variety Rights Act 1987 s. 6.
632. Plant Variety Rights Act 1987 s. 6(4).

homogeneous or that the grant was made to a person who was not the owner of the variety.[633] The Commissioner may cancel a grant before the end of its term.[634]

Decisions of the Commissioner may be appealed to the District Court.[635] If a District Court Judge is satisfied that the appeal involves technical or specialized matters, the Judge can appoint an assessor to sit with the Judge but the assessor does not have power of decision.[636]

§5. Ownership and Transfer (Assignment, Licenses)

194. In order to obtain a grant of a plant variety right, the Commissioner must be satisfied that the applicant for grant is an owner of that variety.[637] The owner in relation to any plant variety, means 'a person who bred or discovered that variety, and includes a successor of that person'.[638]

Where a variety is bred or discovered by two or more persons independently and the Commissioner is satisfied that both of the applicants would otherwise be entitled to a grant, the Commissioner is required to make a grant to the person whose application was made first.[639]

195. A grantee of a plant variety right may assign, mortgage or otherwise dispose of the grant, and the grant may devolve by operation of law.[640] The granted may also license the rights to any other person or persons.[641] The holder of a license from a grantee has the same rights as the grantee to take infringement proceedings.[642]

196. There is also provision for compulsory licenses. Any person may, from three years after grant onwards, request the Commissioner to consider whether reasonable quantities of reproductive material of a reasonable quality of the variety concerned are available for public purchase at a reasonable price.[643] The Commissioner may issue a compulsory license or an order requiring the grantee to sell reproductive material to that person.[644] The Commissioner is required to specify a royalty or payment.[645]

633. Plant Variety Rights Act 1987 s. 15.
634. Plant Variety Rights Act 1987 s. 16.
635. Plant Variety Rights Act 1987 ss 13 and 24.
636. Plant Variety Rights Act 1987 s. 25.
637. Plant Variety Rights Act 1987 s. 10(2).
638. Plant Variety Rights Act 1987 s. 2.
639. Plant Variety Rights Act 1987 s. 11.
640. Plant Variety Rights Act 1987 s. 17(3).
641. Plant Variety Rights Act 1987 s. 17(1)(c).
642. Plant Variety Rights Act 1987 s. 19.
643. Plant Variety Rights Act 1987 s. 21(1).
644. Plant Variety Rights Act 1987 s. 21(2).
645. Plant Variety Rights Act 1987 s. 21(5).

§6. Scope of Exclusive Rights

197. A holder of a grant to a protected variety, or grantee, has the rights set out in section 17 of the Plant Variety Rights Act 1987. The rights of a grantee are proprietary rights.[646]

Section 17 provides that a grantee shall have the exclusive right to produce for sale, and to sell, reproductive material of the variety concerned.[647] The Governor-General may also issue an Order in Council specifying types of plants for which the grantee of a variety right will have the right to propagate that variety for the commercial production of fruit, flowers or other products.[648] Plants currently specified as being plants for which variety rights grant an exclusive right to propagate for commercial production are the following:[649]

- vegetatively propagated fruit-producing plants;
- vegetatively propagated ornamental plants;
- vegetatively propagated vegetable-producing plants.

198. There are exceptions to a grantee's exclusive rights. Any person may propagate, grow or use a protected variety for non-commercial purposes. In addition, if the production of the hybrid or new variety concerned does not require repeated use of that variety, hybridize, or produce a new variety from, a protected variety; or sell any hybrid of, or new variety produced from, a protected variety; or use reproductive material from a protected variety for human consumption or other non-reproductive purposes.[650]

§7. Limitations of the Scope of Protection, Compulsory Licenses

199. Limitations on scope of protection: There are some limitations on the scope of protection granted with a plant variety right. As already noted above, there is an exception to rights allowing any person to propagate, grow or use a protected variety for non-commercial purposes.[651] Hybridization and production of new varieties can also be permitted.[652] It is also not an infringement for people to eat reproductive material from a protected variety, or to use it for other non-reproductive purposes.[653]

There is provision for the Minister responsible for the administration of the Act to impose restrictions on the exercise of a variety right in the public interest during a state of national emergency.[654]

646. Plant Variety Rights Act 1987 s. 17(4).
647. Plant Variety Rights Act 1987 s. 17(1)(a).
648. Plant Variety Rights Act 1987 s. 17(1)(b).
649. Plant Variety Rights (Grantees' Rights) Order 1997 (SR 1997/358) cl. 2.
650. Plant Variety Rights Act 1987 s. 18.
651. Plant Variety Rights Act 1987 s. 18(a).
652. Plant Variety Rights Act 1987 s. 18(b).
653. Plant Variety Rights Act 1987 s. 18(1)(c).
654. Plant Variety Rights Act 1987 s. 17(2).

200. Compulsory Licenses: As already noted, the Plant Variety Rights Act makes provision for compulsory licenses. Other than in the first three years of a grant of rights in a variety, any person may request the Commissioner to consider whether reasonable quantities of reproductive material of a reasonable quality of the variety concerned are available for public purchase at a reasonable price.[655] The Commissioner is required to give the grantee a reasonable time to be heard, and the Commissioner considers any submissions.[656] The Commissioner may issue a compulsory license or an order requiring the grantee to sell reproductive material to that person.[657] The Commissioner is required to specify a royalty or payment.[658]

§8. Duration of Protection

201. The term of protection provided by a grant of a plant variety right is generally twenty-three years for woody plants or rootstock. For other plants, the term is twenty years.[659] The term commences on the day that the right is granted.[660] At the end of the period, the right expires, but it may be cancelled earlier.

A grantee is required to pay an annual grant fee. If the fee is not paid within the period prescribed, the grant may be cancelled.[661]

§9. Infringement and Remedies

202. Section 17 of the Plant Variety Rights Act 1987 sets out the grantee's exclusive rights. The rights are generally the exclusive right to produce for sale and sell reproductive material of the variety, and for fruit, vegetable and ornamental plants, this includes propagation for commercial production of fruit, flowers or other products of the variety.[662] It also provides that propagation, sale or use of imported material as reproductive material without authority constitutes infringement.[663] Importation of produce of a protected variety is also an infringement.[664]

203. It is not an infringement to propagate, grow, or use a protected variety for non-commercial purposes, or, if the production does not require repeated use of the protected variety, to hybridize or produce a new variety from the protected variety.[665] It is also not an infringement to use reproductive material from a protected variety for human consumption or other non-reproductive purposes.[666]

655. Plant Variety Rights Act 1987 s. 21(1).
656. Plant Variety Rights Act 1987 s. 21(2).
657. Plant Variety Rights Act 1987 s. 21(2).
658. Plant Variety Rights Act 1987 s. 21(5).
659. Plant Variety Rights Act 1987 s. 14.
660. Plant Variety Rights Act 1987 s. 14(2).
661. Plant Variety Rights Act 1987 s. 16(2)(g).
662. Plant Variety Rights Act 1987 s. 17(1).
663. Plant Variety Rights Act 1987 s. 17(5).
664. Plant Variety Rights Act 1987 s. 17(6).
665. Plant Variety Rights Act 1987 s. 18(a) and (b).
666. Plant Variety Rights Act 1987 s. 18(c).

204. Section 17 provides that the rights under a grant of a plant variety right are proprietary rights, and their infringement shall be actionable accordingly.[667] Infringement is actionable by the grantee, and the holder of a license from the grantee has the same rights as the grantee to take infringement proceedings.[668] Proceedings may be brought in the District Court or High Court.

Protection commences on the date of grant, and proceedings can be brought from this date.[669] However, there is also provision for provisional protection from the time of application. Section 9 provides that once an application for a grant is made, the applicant has the same rights to take proceedings as if a grant had been made.[670] However if the application is withdrawn, lapses or is declined, then this provisional protection will cease and will be deemed to have never been conferred.[671]

205. Remedies for infringement: Available remedies include interim and permanent injunctions, damages, including exemplary damages, and account of profits. The plaintiff needs to make an election between damages and account of profits as both are not available.

In awarding damages (including any exemplary damages) or granting any other relief, a court is required to take into consideration:[672]

(a) any loss suffered or likely to be suffered by that grantee as a result of that infringement; and
(b) any profits or other benefits derived by any other person from that infringement; and
(c) the flagrancy of that infringement.

There is also a provision for innocent infringement, which applies to damages only. In infringement proceedings, if infringement is established but the defendant can prove that, at the time of the infringement, the defendant was not aware and had no reasonable grounds for supposing that it was an infringement, the plaintiff is not entitled to any damages, but is entitled to an account of profits.[673]

206. Offences: Section 37 of the Plant Variety Rights Act 1987 provides for offences and penalties. Offences include:

- An applicant in an application or attachment supplying any false or misleading information with intent to deceive.[674]
- Falsely representing that any person is the owner of a protected variety or that any person has applied for a grant in respect of any variety.[675]

667. Plant Variety Rights Act 1987 s. 17(4).
668. Plant Variety Rights Act 1987 s. 19.
669. Plant Variety Rights Act 1987 s. 14.
670. Plant Variety Rights Act 1987 s. 9.
671. Plant Variety Rights Act 1987 s. 9(2).
672. Plant Variety Rights Act 1987 s. 17(4).
673. Plant Variety Rights Act 1987 s. 17(8).
674. Plant Variety Rights Act 1987 s. 37(1).
675. Plant Variety Rights Act 1987 s. 37(2).

- Selling material of a variety and falsely representing it is a protected variety or a variety in respect of which an application has been made, or that that material is material of some other variety that is a protected variety or a variety in respect of which an application has been made.[676]
- Wilfully or negligently selling reproductive material without using its denomination.[677]
- Suggesting that a place of business is or is officially connected with the Plant Variety Rights Office.[678]

The penalty for offences is a fine not exceeding NZD 1,000.[679]

§10. Overlapping and Relation to Other Intellectual Property Laws

207. Before the coming into force of the Patents Act 2013, patent protection was also available for plant varieties in New Zealand, but plant varieties were expressly excluded from protection under the new Patents Act.[680]

There is a possibility of overlap between plant variety right infringement and breach of confidence/trade secrets law, if material or information is taken in breach of confidence.[681]

676. Plant Variety Rights Act 1987 s. 37(3).
677. Plant Variety Rights Act 1987 s. 37(4).
678. Plant Variety Rights Act 1987 s. 37(5).
679. Plant Variety Rights Act 1987 s. 37(7).
680. Patents Act 2013 s. 16.
681. *See Franklin v. Giddens* [1978] Qd R 72 (SC).

Chapter 8. Chip Protection

§1. Sources: Legislation

208. In New Zealand, integrated circuits (or chips) are protected by the Layout Designs Act 1994. Copyright protection is not available for layout designs, which are expressly excluded from the definition of artistic work.[682] Layout designs are not excluded from protection in the Patents Act 2013.

The Layout Designs Act was passed in 1994 in the same year as the current Copyright Act. Both statutes were required to fulfil New Zealand's obligations under the TRIPS Agreement. Article 35 of the TRIPS Agreement requires Member countries to protect the layout designs of integrated circuits, incorporating the provisions of the Treaty on Intellectual Property in Respect of Integrated Circuits 1989, and Articles 36–38 detail the scope and term of protection required.

There is effectively no New Zealand case law interpreting the Layout Designs Act 1994. However, the Layout Designs Act 1994 is very similar to the equivalent Australian legislation, the Circuit Layouts Act 1989, and New Zealand courts can be expected to look to Australian case law as required.

Legislation

Layout Designs Act 1994

§2. Subject Matter of Protection

209. The Layout Designs Act 1994 protects layout designs of integrated circuits. To qualify for protection, a layout design must satisfy the definition of 'layout design' in section 2 which provides that:[683]

> 'layout design' means the three-dimensional disposition, however expressed, of the elements, at least 1 of which is an active element, and of some or all of the interconnections, of an integrated circuit; and includes such a three-dimensional disposition prepared for an integrated circuit intended for manufacture.

210. There is a separate definition of 'integrated circuit'. Section 2 defines 'integrated circuit' as:[684]

> a circuit, in its final or an intermediate form, in which the elements, at least 1 of which is an active element, and some or all of the interconnections are integrally

682. Copyright Act 1994 s. 2.
683. Layout Designs Act 1994 s. 2.
684. Layout Designs Act 1994 s. 2.

formed in or on a piece of material and that is intended to perform an electronic function.

211. The Act protects eligible layout designs, so that a layout design must qualify as a layout design under the definition, and also constitute an eligible layout design. To be an 'eligible layout design', a layout design must be original and either one or more of the makers of the layout design must have been an eligible person at the time the layout design was made, or the layout design must have been first commercially exploited in New Zealand or in an eligible country.[685] An 'eligible person' is a New Zealand citizen or body corporate incorporated in New Zealand, or a citizen or body corporate of an eligible country, generally meaning a country that provides protection for layout designs, either under treaty or otherwise.[686]

If a layout design satisfies the requirements to be an eligible layout design, it will be protected subject matter under the Act.

§3. Conditions of Protection

212. To be protected, a layout design must qualify as an eligible layout design. This requires that the layout design must be original, and either one or more of the makers of the layout design must have been an eligible person at the time the layout design was made, or the layout design must have been first commercially exploited in New Zealand or in an eligible country.[687]

I. Original

213. The Act does not define 'original'. However, section 6 provides that, without limiting the ordinary meaning of 'original' in relation to a layout design, a layout design is not original if:[688]

(a) its making involved no intellectual effort by the maker; or
(b) it was commonplace at the time it was made; or
(c) in the case of a combination of elements and interconnections that are commonplace, the combination as a whole involved no intellectual effort by the maker.

This provides some guidance on the meaning of original, and it is clear that not all layout designs will qualify; there is a threshold that requires some quantum of intellectual effort and that the layout design be not commonplace.

685. Layout Designs Act 1994 s. 2.
686. Layout Designs Act 1994 s. 2 and s. 37(1). A list of eligible countries is in the Layout Designs (Eligible Countries) Order 2000.
687. Layout Designs Act 1994 s. 2.
688. Layout Designs Act 1994 s. 6.

II. Qualification

214. A layout design must also qualify as eligible in relation to its maker or first commercial exploitation. The maker of the layout design, for a jointly made layout design anyone or more of the makers, must be an eligible person at the time the layout design was made; or the layout design must be first commercially exploited in New Zealand or in an eligible country.[689]

Section 5 provides that a person who used a computer to make an eligible layout design is to be taken to have made the design, and an eligible layout design is made when it is first fixed in a material form.[690]

An 'eligible person' is a New Zealand citizen or body corporate incorporated in New Zealand, or a citizen or body corporate of an eligible country, generally meaning a country that provides protection for layout designs, either under treaty or otherwise.[691]

'Commercially exploited' is defined in section 3. In summary, a layout design is commercially exploited if the layout design is sold or hired, offered or exposed for sale or hire or imported for sale or hire.[692]

§4. Formalities

215. There are no formalities required for protection. If a layout design qualifies for protection as an eligible layout design then it is protected. In this respect, it is similar to copyright protection.

The Act applies in relation to layout designs which were made either before or after commencement of the Act, but infringement action cannot be brought in respect of acts done before commencement of the Act.[693]

§5. Ownership and Transfer, Assignment, Licenses

216. Ownership: The default rule is that the person who makes an eligible layout design is the first owner of the layout design rights.[694] However, there are exceptions to this rule.

217. The first exception is for employees. Where the person making the layout design makes it under the terms of his or her employment under a contract of service or apprenticeship, the employer is the first owner of the layout design rights in the eligible layout design.[695] This rule can be excluded or modified by agreement.[696]

689. Layout Designs Act 1994 s. 2.
690. Layout Designs Act 1994 s. 5.
691. Layout Designs Act 1994 s. 2 and s. 37(1). A list of eligible countries is in the Layout Designs (Eligible Countries) Order 2000.
692. *See* full definition in Layout Designs Act 1994 s. 3.
693. Layout Designs Act 1994 s. 10.
694. Layout Designs Act 1994 s. 12(1).
695. Layout Designs Act 1994 s. 12(2).
696. Layout Designs Act 1994 s. 12(4).

218. The second exception is for commissioned layout designs. Where a person commissions the making of a layout design for valuable consideration, and the layout design is made in carrying out that commission, commissioner is the first owner of the layout design rights.[697] This rule also can be excluded or modified by agreement.[698]

219. There is also a provision which applies where not all of the makers of the layout design are eligible persons as defined.[699] Where an eligible layout design has been made jointly by persons who are not all eligible persons, the design is treated for ownership purposes as if it had been made solely by those who were eligible persons.[700]

220. Assignment and licenses: Layout design rights are personal property and may be assigned.[701] Future layout design rights may also be assigned.[702] Rights may also pass by will or by operation of law.[703] Assignments may be total or partial. Assignments may be limited to particular classes of exclusive rights, or to a limited period of time.[704] All assignments, whether total or partial, must be in writing and signed by or on behalf of the assignor.[705]

Layout design rights may be licensed by the owner of the rights. The exclusive right to do an act in relation to an eligible layout design, or an integrated circuit made in accordance with an eligible layout design, includes the exclusive right to authorize a person to do that act in relation to that layout design or integrated circuit.[706] Future layout design rights may also be licensed.[707]

Licenses may be exclusive. 'Exclusive license' is defined as:[708]

> a licence in writing, signed by or on behalf of the owner or prospective owner of layout design rights, authorising the licensee, to the exclusion of all other persons, to do an act that, under this Act, the owner would, but for the licence, have the exclusive right to do.

Section 7 provides that an act is done with the license of the owner of the layout design rights if doing that act is authorized by a license binding the owner.[709] Licenses are binding on the grantor's successors in title, except in the case of purchasers in good faith for valuable consideration without notice of the license, or people deriving title from such a purchaser.[710]

697. Layout Designs Act 1994 s. 12(3).
698. Layout Designs Act 1994 s. 12(4).
699. Layout Designs Act 1994 s. 2.
700. Layout Designs Act 1994 s. 12(5).
701. Layout Designs Act 1994 s. 39(1).
702. Layout Designs Act 1994 s. 38. *See also* definition of 'future rights' in sec. 2.
703. Layout Designs Act 1994 s. 39(1).
704. Layout Designs Act 1994 ss 39(2) and 39(3).
705. Layout Designs Act 1994 s. 39(3).
706. Layout Designs Act 1994 s. 4.
707. Layout Designs Act 1994 s. 38. *See also* definition of 'future rights' in sec. 2.
708. Layout Designs Act 1994 s. 2.
709. Layout Designs Act 1994 s. 7.
710. Layout Designs Act 1994 s. 39(4).

§6. Scope of Exclusive Rights

221. Section 13 of the Layout Designs Act 1994 provides that the owner of the layout design rights in an eligible layout design has, during the protection period of the layout design, the following exclusive rights:[711]

(a) the right to copy the layout design, directly or indirectly, in a material form;
(b) the right to make an integrated circuit in accordance with the layout design or a copy of the layout design;
(c) the right to commercially exploit the layout design in New Zealand.

In essence, the exclusive rights are the rights to copy, make an integrated circuit from and commercially exploit the layout design. The exclusive right to do an act in relation to a layout design or integrated circuit includes the exclusive right to authorize a person to do that act in relation to that layout design or integrated circuit.[712]

There is a separate definition of 'commercially exploited'.[713] A layout design is commercially exploited if the layout design, a copy of the layout design or an integrated circuit made in accordance with the layout design is:

(a) sold or hired or otherwise distributed by way of trade; or
(b) offered or exposed for sale or hire or other distribution by way of trade; or
(c) imported for the purpose of sale or hire or other distribution by way of trade.

In addition, a copy of a layout design or an integrated circuit made in accordance with a layout design is commercially exploited in the same circumstances.

§7. Limitations of the Scope of Protection

222. There are no provisions in the Layout Designs Act 1994 for compulsory licensing.

223. There are a number of exceptions to infringement. One of these is for acts done by or on behalf of the Crown or government department for the purposes of defence or national security, or for assisting in a state of national emergency, where all reasonable steps have been taken to obtain a license on reasonable terms.[714] There are limits on the scope of this right.[715] There is a duty to inform the owner of the design rights,[716] and the owner is entitled to remuneration.[717] There is a right of appeal to the High Court.[718]

711. Layout Designs Act 1994 s. 13.
712. Layout Designs Act 1994 s. 4.
713. Layout Designs Act 1994 s. 3.
714. Layout Designs Act 1994 s. 20.
715. Layout Designs Act 1994 s. 21.
716. Layout Designs Act 1994 s. 22.
717. Layout Designs Act 1994 s. 23.
718. Layout Designs Act 1994 s. 24.

§8. Duration of Protection

224. The owner of layout design rights has exclusive rights during the protection period.[719] The 'protection period' is defined as the period beginning on the day on which the layout design was made and ending either:

- if the layout design was first commercially exploited within five calendar years after the calendar year in which the layout design was made, at the end of the tenth calendar year after the calendar year in which the layout design was first commercially exploited; and
- in any other case, at the end of the period of fifteen calendar years after the calendar year in which the layout design was made.[720]

The duration of protection will therefore depend on when the layout design was first commercially exploited, and the period will vary between ten and fifteen years after the layout design was made. Registration or formalities are not required.

§9. Infringement and Remedies

225. Infringement of layout design rights occurs when, during the protection period, a person does, or authorizes another person to do, any act which is the exclusive right of the owner of the layout design right, without the license of the layout design right owner.[721] This means that it is an infringement to copy, make an integrated circuit from, or commercially exploit the layout design without a license from the layout design owner. The doing of an act generally includes doing the act in relation to a substantial part of the design. Copying includes copying of a substantial part and making an integrated circuit from a layout design includes making it from a substantial part of the design.[722]

226. Infringement proceedings may be brought by an owner or exclusive licensee.[723] An exclusive licensee has the same rights and remedies as the owner of the layout design right, and these rights are held concurrently with the owner.[724] The same defences are available against exclusive licensees as against an owner.[725]

227. In infringement proceedings, layout design rights are presumed to subsist in the layout design, and the plaintiff is presumed to be the owner, unless the defendant puts this in issue.[726]

228. There are a number of exceptions to infringement.

719. Layout Designs Act 1994 s. 13.
720. Layout Designs Act 1994 s. 2.
721. Layout Designs Act 1994 s. 14. The exclusive rights are set out in sec. 13.
722. Layout Designs Act 1994 s. 8.
723. Layout Designs Act 1994 ss 25 and 26.
724. Layout Designs Act 1994 s. 28.
725. Layout Designs Act 1994 s. 30.
726. Layout Designs Act 1994 s. 35.

I. Innocent Commercial Exploitation

229. It is not an infringement to commercially exploit or authorize another to commercially exploit, an unauthorized integrated circuit in New Zealand, being an integrated circuit made in accordance with the layout design, which, at the time the person acquired the integrated circuit, the person did not know, and could not reasonably be expected to have known, that the integrated circuit was unauthorized.[727] 'Unauthorized' in this context means an integrated circuit made without the license of the owner of the layout design rights in the layout design.

Commercial exploitation includes sale, hire, distribution and importation for sale hire or distribution.[728] The innocent commercial exploitation exception provides that a person who does any of these things or authorizes someone else to do any of these things, without knowledge, actual or constructive, is not infringing. There is a presumption that such a person did have the requisite knowledge when the layout design, integrated circuit or package or article containing it, is clearly and legibly labelled or marked to indicate that layout design rights subsist and identifying the maker/exclusive licensee and the date first commercially exploited.[729]

II. Copying for Private Use

230. Layout design rights are not infringed by the making of a copy or copies of the layout design or the making of integrated circuits in accordance with the layout design if these are solely for the private use of the person making the copy or copies of the integrated circuit.[730]

It is not private use if the copy or integrated circuit is commercially exploited or distributed otherwise than by way of trade to an extent that will prejudice the interests of the owner of the layout design rights.[731]

III. Copying for Research or Teaching Purposes

231. There is an exception to infringement for the making of a copy or copies of, or the making of an integrated in accordance with, a layout design, if this is solely for research or teaching purposes.[732] There is no definition of 'research' or 'teaching' in the Act, but courts may choose to borrow from the case law on copyright fair dealing exceptions.[733]

727. Layout Designs Act 1994 s. 15.
728. Layout Designs Act 1994 s. 3.
729. Layout Designs Act 1994 s. 36.
730. Layout Designs Act 1994 s. 16(1).
731. Layout Designs Act 1994 s. 16(2).
732. Layout Designs Act 1994 s. 17.
733. Copyright Act 1994 s. 42.

IV. Evaluation or Analysis

232. There is an exception to infringement for making a copy or copies of a layout design for the purposes of evaluating or analysing the layout design. This also extends to an exception to infringement for the making of an original layout design based on such an evaluation or analysis, to making an integrated circuit from, and copying or commercially exploiting that original design.[734] The making of an integrated circuit from a layout design for the purpose of evaluating or analysing the layout design is also permitted, and this also extends to making an original layout design, to making an integrated circuit from, and to copying or commercially exploiting that original layout design.[735]

V. Use for Defence, Security and National Emergency

233. There is a provision exempting from infringement acts done by or on behalf of the Crown or government department for the purposes of defence or national security, or for assisting in a state of national emergency, where all reasonable steps have been taken to obtain a license on reasonable terms.[736] There are limits on the scope of this right.[737] There is a duty to inform the owner of the design rights,[738] and the owner is entitled to remuneration.[739] There is a right of appeal to the High Court.[740]

234. Remedies: Remedies for infringement of rights in a layout design include injunctions, damages and account of profits.[741] Owners of layout design rights and exclusive licensees have the same rights and remedies, held concurrently.[742]

Injunctions are available on the application of the owner or exclusive licensee of layout design rights. Injunctions are to restrain conduct that constitutes, or would constitute, an infringement of the layout design rights.[743]

Damages or an account of profits are generally available in a successful infringement action at the election of the plaintiff.[744] However, where the infringing defendant was not aware and did not have reasonable grounds for suspecting that the act constituted infringement, an account of profits rather than damages may be awarded.[745] Additional damages may be awarded as the court considers appropriate, having regard to the flagrancy of the infringement, any benefit accrued to the defendant because of the infringement and any other relevant matters.[746]

---

734. Layout Designs Act 1994 s. 18(1).
735. Layout Designs Act 1994 s. 18(2).
736. Layout Designs Act 1994 s. 20.
737. Layout Designs Act 1994 s. 21.
738. Layout Designs Act 1994 s. 22.
739. Layout Designs Act 1994 s. 23.
740. Layout Designs Act 1994 s. 24.
741. Layout Designs Act 1994 ss 25–36.
742. Layout Designs Act 1994 s. 28.
743. Layout Designs Act 1994 s. 26.
744. Layout Designs Act 1994 s. 25(1).
745. Layout Designs Act 1994 s. 25(2).
746. Layout Designs Act 1994 s. 25(3).

§10. Overlapping and Relation to Other Intellectual Property Laws

235. There is no overlap between the protection offered by the Layout Designs Act 1994 and protection under the Copyright Act 1994. Copyright protection is not available for layout designs, which are expressly excluded from the definition of artistic work.[747] Layout designs are not excluded from protection in the Patents Act 2013.

747. Copyright Act 1994 s. 2.

Chapter 9. Trade Secrets/Confidential Information

§1. Sources: Legislation

236. In New Zealand law, confidential information or trade secrets are protected through the common law equitable doctrine of breach of confidence.[748] The action for breach of confidence protects confidential information including commercially valuable information or trade secrets. The sources of law are in case law rather than legislation.[749]

However, there is also a criminal provision applying to trade secrets. Section 230 of the Crimes Act 1961 provides as follows:

Taking, obtaining, or copying trade secrets

(1) Every one is liable to imprisonment for a term not exceeding 5 years who, with intent to obtain any pecuniary advantage or to cause loss to any other person,—

(a) dishonestly and without claim of right, takes, obtains, or copies any document or any model or other depiction of any thing or process containing or embodying any trade secret, knowing that it contains or embodies a trade secret; or

(b) dishonestly and without claim of right, takes or obtains any copy of any document or any model or other depiction of any thing or process containing or embodying any trade secret, knowing that it contains or embodies a trade secret.

(2) For the purposes of this section, 'trade secret' means any information that—

(a) is, or has the potential to be, used industrially or commercially; and
(b) is not generally available in industrial or commercial use; and
(c) has economic value or potential economic value to the possessor of the information; and
(d) is the subject of all reasonable efforts to preserve its secrecy.

The broad protection of confidential information is therefore provided by the equitable action of breach of confidence. However, in a much narrower range of cases, the criminal law may apply.

748. *Hunt v. A* [2007] NZCA 332, [2008] 1 NZLR 368, 379.

749. *See* particularly *Coco v. AN Clark (Engineers) Ltd* [1969] RPC 41, *AB Consolidated v. Europe Strength Food Co Pty Ltd* [1978] 2 NZLR 515, *Hunt v. A* [2007] NZCA 332, [2008] 1 NZLR 368.

§2. The Protection of Trade Secrets/Confidential Information

I. The Civil Action

237. The civil action for breach of confidence protects confidential information, irrespective of whether there is a contractual relationship between the parties.[750] The full range of remedies for breach of confidence are available in New Zealand.

Giving the judgment for the New Zealand Court of Appeal in the case of *Hunt v. A.*[751] Hammond J has said that the breach of confidence jurisdiction is based on a broad principle of good faith. The doctrine does not depend upon the existence of a contract between the parties or there being 'property' in the subject matter of the confidence, and it does not depend upon the existence of a fiduciary relationship. Breach of confidence is also not a tort; it is a sui generis cause of action.

238. The breach of confidence action has three elements that are normally required if a case is to succeed outside of a contract. These elements were set out in the case *Coco v. AN Clark Engineers Ltd.*[752] This case has been regularly followed by New Zealand courts.[753] Megarry J said in *Coco v. AN Clark Engineers Ltd.* that:[754]

> [T]hree elements are normally required if, apart from contract, a case of breach of confidence is to succeed. First, the information itself…must 'have the necessary quality of confidence about it'. Secondly, that information must have been imparted in circumstances importing an obligation of confidence. Thirdly, there must be an unauthorised use of that information to the detriment of the party communicating it.

In the New Zealand context, the breach of confidence cause of action was considered by the New Zealand Court of Appeal in the case of *Hunt v. A.*[755] Giving the judgment of the Court, Hammond J said:

> First, the information must be confidential. That is, it must not be something which is publicly known. Secondly, the information must be imparted in circumstances importing an obligation of confidence. This implies some kind of dealings between the parties (not necessarily resulting in a contract). Thirdly, there must have been an unauthorised use of the information. Fourthly, in some circumstances there may be just cause for the use or disclosure of the information. The latter qualification can be traced back to the old equitable maxim that 'there

750. *Saltman Engineering Co Ltd v. Campbell Engineering Co Ltd* (1948) 65 RPC 203.
751. *Hunt v. A* [2007] NZCA 332, [2008] 1 NZLR 368, 379.
752. *Coco v. AN Clark Engineers Ltd* [1969] RPC 41.
753. *See* for example *AB Consolidated v. Europe Strength Food Co Pty Ltd* [1978] 2 NZLR 515, *Hunt v. A* [2007] NZCA 332, [2008] 1 NZLR 368, *Skids Programme Management Ltd v. Barbara Winsome McNeill* [2012] NZCA 314.
754. *Coco v. AN Clark Engineers Ltd* [1969] RPC 41, 47.
755. *Hunt v. A* [2007] NZCA 332, [2008] 1 NZLR 368.

is no confidence in an iniquity', although it was subsequently broadened in the more modern judgments.[756]

A. Necessary Quality of Confidence

239. The first requisite element is that the information must be of a confidential nature. It cannot be public property and public knowledge. However, it can be constructed from materials in the public domain, applying skill and ingenuity to those materials. There must be 'some product of the human brain which suffices to confer a confidential nature upon the information'.[757]

The requirement that the information must be of a confidential nature was discussed by the New Zealand Court of Appeal in *AB Consolidated v. Europe Strength Food Co Pty Ltd.* Woodhouse J said that:[758]

> [T]he mere fact that a concept is a simple one or that the individual or discrete parts of a wider process are publicly known or are used by a trade will not prevent the overall process itself or the concept as a whole from being protected. Nor is it necessary for the information to possess the character of novelty or invention that would be required in the case of a successful patent application.

B. Imparted in Circumstances Importing an Obligation of Confidence

240. In Coco,[759] Megarry J said that the information 'must have been communicated in circumstances importing an obligation of confidence'. It must not be blurted out in public. Megarry J proposed the following test:[760]

> [I]f the circumstances are such that any reasonable man standing in the shoes of the recipient of the information would have realised that upon reasonable grounds the information was being given to him in confidence, then this should suffice to impose upon him the equitable obligation of confidence.

An obligation of confidence is likely to be imposed where commercial or industrial information is given on a business-like basis with a common object such as a joint venture in mind.[761] Megarry J observed however that equity would be unlikely to intervene unless the circumstances are of sufficient gravity, and that 'trivial tittle-tattle' ought not to be protected.

756. Citing *Coco v. AN Clark Engineers Ltd* [1969] RPC 41.
757. *Coco v. AN Clark Engineers Ltd* [1969] RPC 41, 47.
758. [1978] 2 NZLR 515, 521.
759. *Coco v. AN Clark Engineers Ltd* [1969] RPC 41, 47–48.
760. *Coco v. AN Clark Engineers Ltd* [1969] RPC 41, 48.
761. Followed in *Aquaculture Corp v. New Zealand Green Mussel Co Ltd* (1985) 5 IPR 353, 378.

In some cases, a breach of confidence action has applied where there is no relationship of confidence, but rather the confidential information is surreptiously obtained,[762] or there is theft of confidential information.[763]

The obligation of confidence can also extend to third parties. In *Attorney-General v. Guardian Newspapers Ltd (No 2),* Lord Goff said that:[764]

> [A] duty of confidence arises when confidential information comes to the knowledge of a person (the confidant) in circumstances where he has notice, or is held to have agreed, that the information is confidential, with the effect that it would be just in all the circumstances that he should be precluded from disclosing the information to others. I have used the word 'notice' advisedly, in order to avoid the (here unnecessary) question of the extent to which actual knowledge is necessary; though I of course understand knowledge to include circumstances where the confidant has deliberately closed his eyes to the obvious. The existence of this broad principle reflects the fact that there is such a public interest in the maintenance of confidences, that the law will provide remedies for their protection.

This principle was discussed in *Hunt v. A*, where Hammond J in the Court of Appeal reviewed the authorities, and concluded that in the current state of the law in New Zealand the most satisfactory principle to proceed on was to determine whether a third-party recipient of confidential information had acted unconscionably in relation to the acquisition of the information or in the way it had been employed. The factors to be considered in a given case would include: the nature of the information; the state of knowledge of the acquirer of the confidential information; the extent of any breach; what kind of detriment had or might result to other parties; and the degree of 'culpability' of the third-party acquirer and discloser. The most critical factor in the vast majority of cases would be the state of the defendant's knowledge. A third-party recipient with actual knowledge of the confidence likely faced almost insuperable difficulties; as did somebody acting in 'wilful blindness'. The much more problematic areas were constructive knowledge and true 'innocence'.[765]

II. Unauthorized Use

241. The third element is that there must be an unauthorized use of the information. In *Coco*, Megarry J referred to unauthorized use to the detriment of the person communicating it, but noted that there might be cases in which such detriment to the plaintiff did not exist, for example where confidential information gravely injures some relation or friend of the plaintiff.[766]

242. Megarry J also discussed the 'springboard' doctrine. This is the doctrine that a person who has obtained information in confidence has an obligation not to use

762. *See* , e.g., *Douglas and Others v. Hello! Ltd* [2001] QB 967; [2001] 2 All ER 289.
763. *See* , e.g., *Franklin v. Giddins* [1978] Qd R 72.
764. *Attorney-General v. Guardian Newspapers Ltd (No 2)* [1990] 1 AC 109, 281.
765. *Hunt v. A* [2007] NZCA 332, [2008] 1 NZLR 368, 384.
766. *Coco v. AN Clark Engineers Ltd* [1969] RPC 41, 48.

it as a springboard for activities detrimental to the person who gave them the information, and this obligation continues even after the information has become public. Megarry J accepted the principle but had difficulties with the nature and practical effect of the duty imposed. He considered whether it was a duty not to use the information without consent, or a duty not to use the information without paying a reasonable sum for it. He concluded that, in commercial cases such as this, the duty 'seems more likely to be that of not using without paying, rather than of not using at all'.[767] The 'springboard doctrine' also arose in *Aquaculture Corp v. New Zealand Green Mussel Co Ltd*[768] where Prichard J considered the application of the springboard doctrine and the nature of the obligation after the information becomes public. After reviewing the authorities, he suggested that the confidante should not be prevented for all time from using the information, once it is public. He said:[769]

> The remedy, then, is to make him accountable to the person who was the original source of the information – but only to the extent by which he has gained an advantage by virtue of having had information in advance of the general public. Reducing this to practicalities, the advantage unfairly gained can be measured in terms of time saved and, thence, in terms of money.

243. Special cases: The equitable action of breach of confidence requires establishing of three elements. First, the information must be confidential. Second, the information must be imparted or obtained in circumstances importing an obligation of confidence. Third, there must have been an unauthorized use of the information. These are the general principles. There are however special cases, most notably the cases of employees and ex-employees and of government information.

A. Employees and Ex-employees

244. The law of confidential information applying to employees and ex-employees is subject to the terms of the employment contract and relevant principles of employment law. In many cases, the contract of employment will contain express terms relating to confidential information. If there are no express terms, there may nevertheless be implied terms creating obligations of confidence.

The applicable principles were set out in the English Court of Appeal decision in *Faccenda Chicken v. Fowler*.[770] During the course of the employment, there is an implied term imposing a duty of good faith or fidelity on an employee.[771] For ex-employees, the duty to the former employer is more limited. It is clear that ex-employees have a continuing obligation of confidentiality in regard to anything that constitutes

767. *Coco v. AN Clark Engineers Ltd* [1969] RPC 41, 49–50.
768. *Aquaculture Corp v. New Zealand Green Mussel Co Ltd* (1985) 5 IPR 353, 380–385.
769. *Aquaculture Corp v. New Zealand Green Mussel Co Ltd* (1985) 5 IPR 353, 384.
770. *Faccenda Chicken v. Fowler* [1987] 1 Ch 117, 135–138. *See also Nedax Systems NZ Ltd v. Waterford Security Ltd* [1994] 1 ERNZ 491.
771. This duty of good faith is also a statutory duty under the Employment Relations Act 2000 s. 4. *See* discussion in *SGS New Zealand Ltd v. Nortel* (1998) Ltd (High Court, Whangarei, CIV-2006-488-384, 20 Dec. 2007, Winkelmann J).

a trade secret, and this will cover secret processes, formulae, designs, methods or other information sufficiently confidential to constitute a trade secret.[772] This continuing obligation does not cover all information acquired by the employee in the course of employment. It does not cover the general skills, and know-how that is learned, assimilated or enhanced during the employment.[773] It does not cover all information described as 'confidential' during the course of employment, and does not cover information in the public domain.

In determining whether information falls within the implied terms so that it may not be used or disclosed after the employment has ceased, it is necessary to consider all the circumstances of the case.[774] The circumstances to be considered include the nature of the employment, the nature of the information, which must be a trade secret, whether the employer impressed on the employee the confidentiality of the information, and whether the relevant information can be easily isolated from other unprotected information.[775]

The categories of information that can be protected after the termination of employment are not clearly defined. Unless there is a valid restraint of trade clause, an ex-employee may compete with his or her former employer, and this can include contacting or soliciting clients of the former employer. However, difficulties arise in relation to the taking of business and sales information, particularly the taking or memorizing of, customer lists and information. There is authority that a departing employee may not take or memorize customer information for the purposes of competing with the former employer.[776] The departing employee also may not use specialized information about current transactions between employer and customer, ex-employee to compete on unfair terms with the previous employer.[777]

B. Government Information

245. There are particular considerations involved in confidentiality of government information. There is a great deal of government information which is treated as confidential, and some of this is classified. Some categories of information held by government may also attract privacy interests. However, information about the workings of government attract the public interest in a democratic society. The issue was considered by the High Court of Australia in *Commonwealth of Australia v. John Fairfax & Sons Ltd.*[778] In that case, Mason J said that the breach of confidence action had been fashioned to protect personal, private and proprietary interests of the citizen,

772. *Faccenda Chicken v. Fowler* [1987] 1 Ch 117, 136. *See also SSC & B: Lintas New Zealand Ltd v. Murphy* [1986] 2 NZLR 436 (HC).
773. *Nedax Systems NZ Ltd v. Waterford Security Ltd* [1994] 1 ERNZ 491, 505.
774. *Faccenda Chicken v. Fowler* [1987] 1 Ch 117, 137, *Peninsula Real Estate v. Harris* [1992] 2 NZLR 216, 218–219.
775. *Faccenda Chicken v. Fowler* [1987] 1 Ch 117, 137.
776. *Faccenda Chicken v. Fowler* [1987] 1 Ch 117, 136, *Peninsula Real Estate v. Harris* [1992] 2 NZLR 216, 218–219.
777. *SSC & B: Lintas New Zealand Ltd v. Murphy* [1986] 2 NZLR 436 (HC).
778. *Commonwealth of Australia v. John Fairfax & Sons Ltd* (1980) 147 CLR 39 (HCA).

not the very different interests of the executive government. Government is supposed to act in the public interest. Mason J said:[779]

> It may be a sufficient detriment to the citizen that disclosure of information relating to his affairs will expose his actions to public discussion and criticism. But it can scarcely be a relevant detriment to the government that publication of material concerning its actions will merely expose it to public discussion and criticism. It is unacceptable in our democratic society that there should be a restraint on the publication of information relating to government when the only vice of that information is that it enables the public to discuss, review and criticize government action.

Accordingly, the Court will determine the government's claim to confidentiality by reference to the public interest. Unless disclosure is likely to injure the public interest, it will not be protected.

Mason J said that information would not be protected if it merely threw light on the past workings of government, but it would be protected if disclosure would be contrary to the public interest because it would prejudice national security, relations with foreign countries or the ordinary business of government.[780]

Similar considerations were raised in the New Zealand Court of Appeal in *Attorney-General for the UK v. Wellington Newspapers Ltd,*[781] a case involving disclosures about the workings of government security services. The Court took a similar approach to that taken in *Commonwealth of Australia v. John Fairfax & Sons Ltd,* balancing the conflicting considerations of confidentiality and public interest in disclosure, albeit in the context of the public interest defence.

C. Defences

246. Public Interest Defence: There is a public interest defence to breach of confidence. This defence is based on the idea that 'there is no confidence as to the disclosure of iniquity'.[782] Iniquity in this context includes crime, fraud, misdeeds and breaches of national security.[783] Establishing the public interest defence requires a defendant to show that the public interest in disclosure outweighs the public interest in confidentiality.[784] In *Attorney-General for the UK v. Wellington Newspapers Ltd,* McMullin J said that:[785]

> By public interest is meant something more than that which catches one's curiosity or merely raises the interest of the gossip. It is something which may be of real concern to the public.

---

779. *Commonwealth of Australia v. John Fairfax & Sons Ltd* (1980) 147 CLR 39, 51–52 (HCA).
780. *Commonwealth of Australia v. John Fairfax & Sons Ltd* (1980) 147 CLR 39, 52 (HCA).
781. *Attorney-General for the UK v. Wellington Newspapers Ltd* [1988] 1 NZLR 129 (CA).
782. *Gartside v. Outram* (1856) 26 LJ Ch 113, 114, Wood V-C.
783. *Attorney-General for the UK v. Wellington Newspapers Ltd* [1988] 1 NZLR 129, 178 (CA).
784. *Lion Laboratories Ltd v. Evans* [1984] 2 All ER 417.
785. *Attorney-General for the UK v. Wellington Newspapers Ltd* [1988] 1 NZLR 129, 178 (CA).

The public interest defence has been argued in New Zealand cases.[786] Disclosure of confidential information about wrongdoing by the security services of the UK, being a country to which New Zealand was aligned and from which New Zealand's own security service was initially recruited, was protected by the public interest.[787] The defence was also relied on in a case relating to disclosure of the confidential business plans of a state-owned enterprise,[788] and in a case relating to disclosures of confidential transactions by foreign companies designed to avoid tax.[789] In some cases, there may be a public interest in publication, but only to the relevant authorities rather than to the public generally.

247. Defence of Prior Publication: There is also a defence of prior publication. This defence applies if the information is already so widely publicized that it is already in the public domain and is no longer confidential.[790] The defence applies where the material has already been published to such extent so as to destroy confidentiality, and this publication has been by someone other than the defendant. The extent of publication required is a matter of degree.[791]

248. Remedies: Remedies in actions for breach of confidence include injunctions, both interim and permanent, Anton Pillar orders and damages.

III. Criminal Offences

249. In 2003, a criminal provision applying to trade secrets was introduced into the Crimes Act 1961.

Section 230 of the Crimes Act 1961 provides as follows:

Taking, obtaining, or copying trade secrets

(1) Every one is liable to imprisonment for a term not exceeding 5 years who, with intent to obtain any pecuniary advantage or to cause loss to any other person,—

(a) dishonestly and without claim of right, takes, obtains, or copies any document or any model or other depiction of any thing or process containing or embodying any trade secret, knowing that it contains or embodies a trade secret; or

(b) dishonestly and without claim of right, takes or obtains any copy of any document or any model or other depiction of any thing or process containing or embodying any trade secret, knowing that it contains or embodies a trade secret.

(2) For the purposes of this section, 'trade secret' means any information that—

786. *See* for example *Blum v. ANZ Bank New Zealand Ltd* [2015] NZCA 335.
787. *Attorney-General for the UK v. Wellington Newspapers Ltd* [1988] 1 NZLR 129.
788. *New Zealand Post Ltd v. Prebble* [2001] NZAR 360 (HC).
789. *European Pacific Banking Corp v. Fourth Estate Publications Ltd* [1993] 1 NZLR 559 (HC).
790. *Attorney-General for the UK v. Wellington Newspapers Ltd* [1988] 1 NZLR 129, 179 (CA).
791. *Attorney-General for the UK v. Wellington Newspapers Ltd* [1988] 1 NZLR 129, 175 (CA).

(a) is, or has the potential to be, used industrially or commercially; and
(b) is not generally available in industrial or commercial use; and
(c) has economic value or potential economic value to the possessor of the information; and
(d) is the subject of all reasonable efforts to preserve its secrecy.

The broad protection of confidential information is therefore provided by the equitable action of breach of confidence. However in a much narrower range of cases, the criminal law may apply. The definition of 'trade secret' in section 230(2) is much narrower than that applying in the broader civil action. The criminal provision is focussed only on industrial or commercial information with economic value.

There are as yet no cases on this section. There is considerable potential for this provision to be used in cases involving the taking of commercially valuable information, for example by departing employees. The available penalty is imprisonment for a term not exceeding five years.

In addition to section 230, section ss 248–254 of the Crimes Act set out crimes involving computers, all carrying a prison term. These include an offence of damaging or interfering with a computer system (section 250), an offence of accessing a computer system without authorization, (section 252) and an offence of accessing a computer system for a dishonest purpose (section 249). Cases involving the taking of information have been prosecuted under these other computer misuse provisions, particularly section 249(1) which prohibits accessing a computer system for a dishonest purpose.[792] Section 249 provides for up to seven years imprisonment for directly or indirectly accessing any computer system and, dishonestly or by deception, and without claim of right, obtaining any property, privilege, service, pecuniary advantage, benefit, or valuable consideration; or causing loss to any other person. Under this provision, there is no need to show that a document has been taken, obtained or copied. There is no need to establish that any information taken meets the definition of a 'trade secret' as in section 230. In addition, section 249(2) prohibits directly or indirectly accessing any computer system *having the intent* to do any of the acts in section 249(1), and is directed at attempts.

---

792. *See* for example *Watchorn v. R* [2014] NZCA 493, *Dixon v. R* [2015] NZSC 147.

Chapter 10. Geographical Indications and Appellations of Origin

250. For the purposes of the TRIPS Agreement, Geographical Indications are indications which identify a good as originating in the territory of a Member, or a region or locality in that territory, where a given quality, reputation or other characteristic of the good is essentially attributable to its geographical origin.[793]

As a signatory to the TRIPS Agreement, New Zealand is required to provide the legal means for interested parties to prevent the use of geographical indications in a manner which misleads the public as to the geographical origin of the good; and any use which constitutes an act of unfair competition.[794] Additional protection is required for geographical indications for wines and spirits, preventing the use of geographical indications for goods not originating from that place, even where the true origin of the goods is indicated or the geographical indication is used in translation or accompanied by expressions such as 'kind', 'type', 'style', 'imitation' or the like.[795]

251. New Zealand does not have a sui generis regime to cover all geographical indication protection. Protection is provided to geographical indications through a mix of general regimes, and specific legislation for wines and spirits only.

252. The Fair Trading Act 1986 protects against misleading conduct in trade. Section 9 provides that 'No person shall, in trade, engage in conduct that is misleading or deceptive or is likely to mislead or deceive.' Misleading use of geographical indications may therefore constitute a breach of the Fair Trading Act.[796]

253. The tort of passing off also provides protection for geographical indications in circumstances where the requirements of the tort are met. A plaintiff in a passing off action needs to show that there is some reputation or goodwill attached to its name, mark or get-up, that the defendant has used the same or a deceptively similar name, mark or get-up so as to confuse or deceive the relevant public or if unrestrained is likely to do so, and that as a result damage has been or is likely to plaintiff's business.[797] The tort of passing off has been successfully used in New Zealand to protect a geographic indication, in a case where the French producers of champagne sought to prevent the use of 'champagne' by Australian wine producers selling sparkling white wine in New Zealand.[798]

254. Geographical indications can also be protected as a collective or certification trade mark in New Zealand, under the Trade Marks Act 2002, so long as statutory

793. Agreement on Trade Related Aspects of Intellectual Property Rights 1994 (TRIPS Agreement), Art. 22(1).
794. Agreement on Trade Related Aspects of Intellectual Property Rights 1994 (TRIPS Agreement), Art. 22(2).
795. Agreement on Trade Related Aspects of Intellectual Property Rights 1994 (TRIPS Agreement), Art. 23.
796. *Tot Toys Ltd v. Mitchell* [1993] 1 NZLR 325, 367(HC).
797. *Tot Toys Ltd v. Mitchell* [1993] 1 NZLR 325, 334 (HC).
798. *Wineworths Group Ltd v. Comite Interprofessional Du Vin De Champagne* [1992] 2 NZLR 327 (CA).

requirements are met.[799] A trade mark containing a protected geographical indication may not be registered in relation to goods that do not originate from the place indicated by the geographic indication.[800]

255. In relation to wines and spirits, there is a specific statute, the Geographical Indications (Wine and Spirits) Registration Act 2006, but the Act is not yet in force. In the Act, a 'geographical indication' is defined as an 'indication that identifies a wine or spirit as originating in the territory of a country, or a region or locality in that territory, where a given quality, or reputation, or other characteristic, of the wine or spirit is essentially attributable to its geographical origin'.[801] Once in force, this Act will establish a registration system for wine and spirit geographical indications and provide for some limitations and exceptions. In 2014 the government agreed to implement the Act, and the Geographical Indications (Wine and Spirits) Registration Amendment Bill was introduced to Parliament in November 2015.

799. Trade Marks Act 2002 s. 5.
800. Trade Marks Act 2002 s. 20.
801. Geographical Indications (Wine and Spirits) Registration Act 2006 s. 6.

Selected Bibliography

§1. Books

Ian Finch (ed.). *James & Wells Intellectual Property Law in New Zealand.* 2nd edn. Brookers Ltd, 2012.
Susy Frankel. *Intellectual Property in New Zealand.* 2nd edn. LexisNexis, 2011.
Anna Kingsbury. *Butterworths Student Companion: Intellectual Property.* 2nd edn. LexisNexis, 2012.
Paul Sumpter. *Intellectual Property Law: Principles in Practice.* 2nd edn. CCH, 2013.
Paul Sumpter. *Trade Marks In Practice* 3rd edn. LexisNexis, 2015.
Stephen Todd (ed.). *The Law of Torts in New Zealand.* 7th edn. Brookers Ltd 2016.

§2. Journals

John Lulich, *New Zealand Intellectual Property Journal.* LexisNexis.

§3. Legal Encylopedias

Sir Robin Cooke, *Laws of New Zealand: Intellectual Property.* LexisNexis, 1992–.

§4. Looseleaf Services and Databases

Clive Elliott et al., *Intellectual Property in New Zealand: Copyright and Design.* ed. John Lulcih LexisNexis, 1996.
Ian Finch (ed.). *Intellectual Property Law in New Zealand.* Westlaw NZ: Brookers Ltd.

§5. Waitangi Tribunal Report

Waitangi Tribunal. *Ko Aotearoa Tēnei: A Report into Claims Concerning New Zealand Law and Policy Affecting Māori Culture and Identity*: Wai 262, Waitangi Tribunal Report, 2011.

Selected Bibliography

Index

The numbers here refers to paragraph numbers.

Index

Made in the USA
Monee, IL
18 October 2026

66037596R10098